What If You Live?

What If You Live?

The Truth about Retiring in the
Early 21st Century 2nd Edition

Paul M. Gargano, CFP®

WHAT IF YOU LIVE?
THE TRUTH ABOUT RETIRING IN THE
EARLY 21ST CENTURY 2ND EDITION

iUniverse books may be ordered through booksellers or by contacting:

iUniverse
1663 Liberty Drive
Bloomington, IN 47403
www.iuniverse.com
1-800-Authors (1-800-288-4677)

Because of the dynamic nature of the Internet, any web addresses or links contained in this book may have changed since publication and may no longer be valid. The views expressed in this work are solely those of the author and do not necessarily reflect the views of the publisher, and the publisher hereby disclaims any responsibility for them.

Any people depicted in stock imagery provided by Thinkstock are models, and such images are being used for illustrative purposes only.
Certain stock imagery © Thinkstock.

ISBN: 978-1-4917-6901-0 (sc)
ISBN: 978-1-4917-6900-3 (e)

Library of Congress Control Number: 2015908805

Print information available on the last page.

iUniverse rev. date: 06/25/2015

CONTENTS

Acknowledgement

For my father, Anthony Gargano, the greatest man I've ever known…
For my mother, Ruth Gargano, the smartest mom I've ever known…
For my wonderful children, Hanna, Anthony and Ashleigh…
And most of all, for my darling bride Donna,
with whom I look forward to enjoying a long,
relaxing and healthy retirement.

A special thanks to Marianne Linker for editing my book.

Find your favorite place to sit down and relax……. Imagine this for a minute………

You're on the beach in early summer sitting about twenty feet from the ocean feeling a cool breeze off your left shoulder. You're calm, content, and totally at ease about everything in life.

You're eyes are closed as you rest and relax on one of those very comfortable beach chairs . . . *you feel fantastic.*

You're wearing an awesome pair of sunglasses that you recently purchased.

One of those oversized beach hats is on your head, blocking the sun from your face.

You can hear your grandchildren in the background running on the beach while they're laughing.

Your son and daughter-in-law are laying next to you whispering tender words and having fun.

Your husband gently touches your shoulder as he hands you a refreshment, then lays down next to you.

As you think for a moment, you begin to realize… you don't have a care in the world when it comes to money and finances…………………………… *you're having a wonderful life.*

If this vision seems like something you'd like in your future…..keep reading.

INTRODUCTION

What if you live?

Wow, I can't believe that it's been five years since my first edition of **"What If You Live?"** It's amazing that the concepts in this book are becoming normal conversation for many today. I recently listened to a radio guru discuss my ideas as if they were his own. Retirement comprises of having a great "second half of life" while maintaining the lifestyle that you have always dreamed and hoped for.

My theory in this book involves producing a customized solution for each individual family so that they can live a stress free retirement. This arch of protection and growth is so specialized that each person's plan (fleet of ships) is made-to-order. This **"Multiple Boat Theory"** helps families retire and prepare for any type of market condition from calm seas to rough seas … even hurricanes. In plain terms: when you retire, you must be prepared for a simple market downturn, a long bear market, or another "Great Depression!"

For many, they just don't get it. Financial Professionals along with a multitude of Americans, feel that they can manage a retirement future by following the norm. If the retiree is a do-it-yourselfer, they just follow a web site, use some kind of investment model, or choose what their neighbor tells them at a party might be a good pick. If this account gets larger, they feel like a genius. When the account begins to fall, fear takes over, they become disoriented, and don't know what to do. This is the point when having a plan in place, along with the help of a CFP® professional that is totally committed to their success, becomes so important.

What is the process today for the average Financial Professional when they help a client invest and plan for retirement? They install a proprietary system and place their client into one large brokerage account. They diversify according to risk; and still watch the portfolio fall dramatically during market downturns. At this point, they call their client once a year to say "the market is long term … just hold on … you will be fine." Let's look closer at the word **"fine."** Webster's definition is "exceptional." I don't know about you, but looking at a thirty percent loss in a retirement portfolio is anything but…**exceptional!**

A common question that I receive today: **"are we heading for a market downturn?"** The easy answer is "yes, of course…but I don't know when." For the readers that don't know my portfolio management concepts, this will help to educate them. Major market swings happen more often than people realize. The average thirty percent fall in the markets is normal. In the past, major upswings were accompanied with large downswings. The problem with most investors during major market downswings is that they retreat **(sell low)** and possibly never return. Or more often than not, they move back in after the markets have already peaked **(buy high)** just before another downward move. This is a recipe for disaster.

Now, I know that some of my theories in this book are complicated; but, if you'll take the time to read it in its entirety, work on your personal budget, and place these concepts into your own world . . . I believe this book may help you to succeed and live a great retirement….. *So, read on and enjoy!*

While thinking about the word **"retirement,"** what comes to mind for most Americans? Webster's Dictionary defines it as "withdrawal from one's occupation or position; concludes one's career." It doesn't bother to define retirement as a successful or unsuccessful venture. It doesn't imply the possible complications through this last phase of life. The fact that Americans are attempting to successfully live for up to thirty years without having to work isn't even mentioned. If I were to bring you to the peak of Mount Everest, have you look over the edge, and then tell you "step off," wouldn't your first and only concern be the consequences? I would hope so! The fall may not kill you. However, the sudden stop surely would; and retirement is a sudden stop. It's the completion to the working life that you have grown accustomed to. *"What if you live?"*

Retirement today could be defined as living on the beach, carefree, happy, and drinking margaritas. It could also be defined as a daily struggle; worrying about how long your life savings will last; tormented about how much income you should take from your savings every single month;

concerned if you're investing correctly, and questioning if you should go out and get a job. What a way to live.

This book was written for the concerned and frustrated retirees or **"soon to be"** retirees. It was written for those that have worked hard and care about their future. Waking up at age seventy five and looking at a zero balance on your account statements is a nightmare for all retirees. Living on social security alone is no way to live and having to go out and get a job in your later years can be devastating. Everyone needs a customized plan in place.

I have been helping families since the late nineties and believe that the book you are about to read will be the most important book that you've ever picked up concerning retirement. I know that I'm biased when it comes to my investment philosophy, but you'll have to admit that the investment and retirement world of today is in shambles. Many Americans don't know what to do.

I have been recognized as an accomplished speaker and author in the United States. I am also one of the top Retirement Planners in North Carolina and have been Rated Best of Charlotte, N.C. for multiple years. I don't believe in the norm when it comes to your retirement. The "buy and hold" concepts of the past are dead. I have a distinct investment philosophy, I call it the "multiple boats theory" or MBT. This concept is unique, innovative, and I feel "a must" for the majority of retirees. These ideas involve a plan for protection and growth to help Americans reach their goals. These programs are customized to each individual because everyone has a different viewpoint on risk and reward. **Wake up.....you are in trouble!**

The hard truth is that the next fifty years of our society will face some of the most difficult times that current generations have ever seen. Social Security, Medicare, and other trusted retirement plans may not provide the anticipated benefits—**probably won't** provide the anticipated benefits! Most individuals do not realize their personal responsibility and opportunity to develop customized plans until it is too late. Yet, with the proper planning now, you can significantly increase the likelihood that you will be able to live in a comfortable lifestyle in your retirement and twilight years. Because after all...*what if you live?*

THE FINE PRINT
(aka the Legal Mumbo Jumbo)

The views expressed in this book are those of Paul M. Gargano, CFP® or GARGANO and should not be construed as investment advice. All information is believed to be from reliable sources; however, we make no representation as to its completeness or accuracy. Asset allocation, which is driven by complex mathematical models, should not be confused with diversification, a much simpler concept. Neither asset allocation, diversification, strategic management, tactical management, systematic investing, dollar cost averaging, account rebalancing, nor alternative asset classes, can assure a profit or protect against loss. All economic and performance information is historical or hypothetical and not indicative of future results. Please consult your representative for more information. *What if You Live? The Truth About Retiring in The Early Twenty-First Century 2ⁿᵈ Edition* does not sponsor, promote, sell, or endorse any insurance company, corporation, investment firm, banking institution, advisory team, or the products and services they provide.

CHAPTER 1

Retirement Today

It's late at night and the moon is full. You are driving your family to the local train station. A light mist of fog starts rolling into the low lying streets and there is a definite chill in the air. As you pull into the station parking lot you are amazed at what you see. Before you is a train station that looks as if it came from the era of the thirties. The setting is dark and gloomy with the distant sound of wolves coming from the nearby forest.

Your family enters and begins to walk through the station looking for the ticket counter. There are many different types of families in line with you as you purchase tickets for your journey. Each family seems to be looking forward to the trip as they enjoy each other's company.

As you begin to board the train, the first thing you notice is the massive size and length of this vehicle; it seems to go on forever. Walking down the aisle you notice that all the seats face backwards. Your family quickly takes their seats and awaits their journey. The name of this train is **"Retirement."**

Most passengers are riding this train content and unaware of their dooming consequences. Facing backwards allows them to judge their fate by looking at the past not the present or the future. They are living only in the moment and not preparing for the possibility of living over thirty years in retirement.

Looking ahead, we can see that the bridge ten miles down the track is out. This bridge stands high over a mountain valley thousands of feet from the ground below. For most, this future "train wreck" will totally destroy their dreams of retirement. They will end up working a menial job through their seventies and possibly eighties just to survive. For some, they will have prepared for this day, survive the tragedy, and enjoy their later retirement years.

This analogy may seem trite, but the consequences are real and the future is not guaranteed. Americans are in trouble and they need to get moving when it comes to future planning. **WAKE UP AMERICA!** The current task of managing retirement money has changed forever. If you try to manage your retirement assets using what I call "the norm" today, I feel you will inevitably end up at the bottom of that mountain valley. Let's take a look at some new ideas.

This book is built around an analogy I developed years ago about investing. I call it the **"Multiple Boat Theory"** or MBT. Based on many years of experience and observation, I believe that most individuals are investing today using antiquated ideas. They are literally sailing the seas on a long journey in a centuries-old sailboat going back in time 500 years. *(Yes, 500 years.)* The captain of this boat uses only the stars for direction and has little knowledge of awaiting storms or hurricanes. The inevitable future for this boat's journey is literally.... a guess! The many market crashes in the past two decades help to prove my point. *Normal investing today won't work for retirees.*

It doesn't take much to imagine the fear that those individuals felt years ago sitting below deck in a storm in this centuries old sailboat: passengers being tossed like fine crystal, hearing only the sounds of the waves crashing against the hull, and seeing only the constant fear in each other's eyes. They didn't know their future and they feared their destiny along with the destiny of their children and their belongings. Everything that they owned usually accompanied them on this journey. For the investor today…this current voyage involves only their life savings, not their lives; but, is there really a difference when you're looking at your entire financial future?

Wouldn't you agree that many investors today are riding in *only one large sailboat*. Maybe a 401k or IRA that is in a single brokerage account. Possibly using many types of stocks or bonds but not using different types of vehicles. Many Americans are afraid to look at their future retirement situation? They don't even open up their statements; and if they did, most wouldn't know how to evaluate them. They wake up at age sixty and say to themselves *"What should I do?"*

My philosophy involves owning many diverse types of boats that move in different ways. These boats are designed to handle multiple situations while helping to provide a worry free retirement:

- A modern day Sailboat with an array of weather equipment that can analyze storms ahead and hopefully make your journey a successful one.
- A Nuclear Submarine designed to submerge deep underwater, unaffected by the market turmoil and storms above.
- A Speedboat that is designed to go fast and make excessive returns if the weather permits.
- An Aircraft Carrier designed to handle the stormy seas and have many types of aircraft that can reach a multiple of shores. (Hopefully dispersing dividends.)

Let's look at some numbers:

This combination is useful for any investor, but especially for the retiree that must avoid the **"perfect storm."** This storm involves three different events happening at the same time. These three variables are current income need, bear market, and inflation. In the following example the retiree's income need is 6% of $100,000 or $6,000 per year.

I want to preface this by stating that in order to keep this simple, let's look at a short term scenario of two years. During a "perfect storm" of income withdrawals, inflation, and a market loss, the negative effect is greatly exaggerated. The goal is to get the retirement account back to where it began (including the inflation factor) by the end of the *second year* in order to stop a possible account and retirement collapse.

In this example, we are starting with $100,000 and working with 3% inflation. The account needs to grow by 3% per annum. At the end of the second year this account should equal approximately $106,090 by factoring inflation. I can't stress the importance of this enough because if this account value keeps falling; your retirement is over!

First year:

- $100,000 minus 33% market loss = $67,000
- $67,000 minus income of $6,000 = $61,000 = value at end of first year
- $61,000 minus income of $6,000 = $55,000 = value at end of second year if zero growth
- $55,000 needs to almost double in order to equal $106,090. We need a return of approximately 100% to get back to where we started. **What are the odds on that?**

The conclusion is this: In a normal scenario, when withdrawing a 6% income stream, a **33% loss needs approximately a 100% gain** by the end of the second year, to reach the appropriate inflation adjusted account balance. A **20% loss needs an approximate 60% gain**. A **5% loss needs an approximate 28% gain**; yes . . .28%. I hate to be redundant; but do you get the point? Any loss in retirement is unacceptable. I don't care if you own only conservative investments, loss is always possible! Are you beginning to see the importance of money management during retirement?

Most investors may believe that a market loss of 33% needs a market gain of 33% . . . wow what a mistake in a "perfect storm". A 33% loss needs approximately a 100% gain just to get back to even in the second year. **PREPARE OR PERISH!!!**

For the skeptics out there that are thinking they would just invest in CDs at that point in life; I will reply by writing, be very careful of the "silent killer": inflation. Let's take a quick look.

First year:

- $100,000 plus 2% conservative investment = $102,000
- $102,000 minus income of $6,000 = $96,000 = value at the end of first year
- $96,000 plus 2% conservative investment = $97,920
- $97,920 minus income of $6,000 = $91,920 = value at the end of the second year
- $91,920 needs to grow by over 15% to achieve $106,090. Do you really think you can attain a 15% return in CD's? Inflation would be flying! Eventually, your retirement is over ... **back to work!**

Each year your account would be decreasing. Even if you assume that your return may increase to more than 2%, I would contend that in periods of high fixed returns we have high inflation. Eventually, your account's true worth would diminish to zero. Living twenty to thirty years in retirement may then require much sacrifice and outside income. Thus my quote, ***"What if you live?"***

Your homework:

- Work on your budget for your retirement years.
- Get your statements together.
- Write down your investments and the dollar values.
- Calculate the total percentages.
- Are any investments a large portion of your portfolio? Should they be?
- Find a CFP˚ professional in your town to help plan your future.

CHAPTER 2

Throw the Investment Game Book Away

Americans have found themselves in a new world when it comes to investing and retirement planning. The era of "buy and hold" is dead and the "old game book" no longer applies. We would be naïve to believe that we can rely on what happened in the past as a predictor for what will happen in the future, but we <u>can</u> use the lessons of our youth to guide us in making the right long-term decisions.

This chapter will discuss the following areas:

- The 'Good Old' Days
- When You're Family
- Plain Vanilla Investing
- Me, Myself, and I
- Bull vs. Bear Market
- Beware the Bag of Gold
- Milk vs. Mail
- Investment Philosophy Today
- What Your Retirement Means
- Loss
- Retirement Tax Planning- A Moving Target
- Ten Questions to Ask an Advisor

The 'Good Old' Days

Hopefully, the readers of this book can look back on fantastic joy-filled childhoods with an abundance of imaginations and plenty of love from family and friends. Youth can certainly be a wondrous and remarkable— yet unfortunately fleeting time. As adults, we endeavor everyday to savor those precious memories of the past—especially when times get tough. Our cocooned young lives did not see the harsh realities of the "real world," and was therefore artificially perfect. Adults get to deal with reality, although frankly, the world of today is in many ways an even more uncharitable place than the one our parents had to face as adults.

Think back to a time when you were a small child tucked into that comfy bed nightly by loving parents. The feelings of awe and anticipation on Christmas Eve as you waited for Santa Claus to arrive with a bag full of presents. You wondered with expectation and amazement as to what time he might arrive. Maybe you would have the chance to hear him sneak down the chimney, or possibly get a chance to see his fabled sled and reindeer—**wow!** Those were the days of mystery, excitement, wonder, and passion. Oh, what a wonderful life! Now we wish the same for our children, and grandchildren—to have that spark, delight, and pure glee that should come with youth.

For the retiree of today, those glorious days of old that represented the comfort and joy of childhood also brought a remarkable world of hope and dreams. Growing up, our friends and family meant everything to us, and we to them. Today, we cherish the photos and mementos of those memories. I have to laugh sometimes when I walk into the popular chain restaurant **"Cracker Barrel"** and ponder the actual importance of all the pictures and memorabilia hung carelessly on the walls. On every wall hangs aged posters, photos, tools, road signs…all affixed in drywall as mere decoration—to enhance a theme. And yet, I have a delightfully spry eighty year old client who absolutely loves to go to Cracker Barrel. All of that "decoration" reminds him of a past; a gentler time, a moment in his life filled with peace and happiness. To him the traditional pictures are reminiscent of his youth, past friendships long lost and forgotten family. To the restaurant manager, the wait staff, and the owners; those things are there to set a frame of mind, and they do. They represent a happier time of hope and promise. He is comfortable there among the memorabilia—even if it's not his own.

The 'good old' days were a great time. And in so many ways, it is natural to be nostalgic about a time when things were seemingly so right in the world. It is ok to hang on to the feelings and memories that time conjures—and want that purity and joy to be a part of your retirement.

When You're Family

As we grow from small children into young adults, our feelings of "family" sometimes become so deeply ingrained in our personality—we literally become the sum of the relatives around us. "Family" even becomes a word that means more than it does on the surface. The phrase: "treated as family" was very common in my youth. To be treated "just like family" was expected in many circumstances—be it at a friend's home, or at the corner grocery. And treating others in this manner—welcoming, caring, open, was reciprocated. This is how I was raised, and the same was probably true for you as well. Now as older adults, we look for these mutually fulfilling symbiotic relationships in our business and personal matters. We are comforted when people in our lives are the kind of people that protect us, look out for our best interest and care about us—who are "family."

In those grand days of our past, we could easily walk into the neighborhood bank and request a loan just based solely on our promise of repayment. If we had good standing in the community and gave "our word" that we would make every effort to pay back the loan on time, and with interest, this was enough. Years ago, "our word" was something valued and valuable… something of which many of today's children have no comprehension (probably because they are not shown it by example). Their world is not always the one of anticipation and hope; but rather they see the world, the government, and the businesses around them not living up to their promises. It was the iconic John Wayne, who first put the popularized "a man's word" as being something sacred and celebrated in the movies. However, it was my father who made it a part of who I am! Oh, what a marvelous time to be a child and to grow up!

Put plainly, today we live in a cold adult world of numbers and penalties. Our word has little value when it comes to things like promising to repay a loan. Nor can we always trust someone else who makes promises to us. Gone as well, is the youthful wonder, passion, excitement, and the universal feeling that our families extend beyond our households and genetic code. No longer can you get a loan from a neighborhood banker on your word. In fact, we no longer even recognize our neighborhood banker, or them, us! We live in a world where a bank is a big faceless institution full of hoards of dispassionate employees. These employees are held only to deadlines, bank fees, statistics, and goals in place of customer service, and a sense of community. In too many cases, banks no more attempt to have a relationship of trust with their clients. They no longer treat us like "family"... **that word means nothing to them!**

Even in this fast-food, fast-service, fast-track new reality, you have to admit: relationships are still important. They are not always valued, but they **ARE** important. This may have been forgotten by our banks, the check-out person at the grocery store, and the kid delivering our newspaper. However, if you want to be confident in your financial decisions, the relationship between you and your Financial Professional is crucial, and should be valued.

If you care about the relationship between you and the people with whom you trust with your money, investments, and future; you do still have a choice. You can choose an Advisor Associate who is independent, with a bank, or large brokerage house. The best choice will always be the one where your Financial Professional is true to their word, who knows you and your goals, and who wants to partner with you and put your interests first at all times. Who will you trust to make the decisions about your money and your future? Do you want an advisor that comes to your home, treats you like family, gives you his word and stands behind it? Alternatively, will you choose this person because he works for a large company with a big name? **I hope that you've been reading!**

Plain Vanilla Investing

In early 2008, I sat down with a widow who was upset with her Financial Professional. It seems she had walked into her local bank with her life savings. The young advisor showed her four stocks to buy and position her money. **Only four stocks!** This poor woman lost 25% in just a few short weeks and didn't know what to do. She was devastated—and so was her retirement money.

I recently sat with a divorcee that was positioned into the opposite spectrum by her Financial Professional, 100% bonds. This Advisor Associate that she had chosen four years ago after her divorce, installed her into an allocation of total bonds without even trying to calculate her future investment needs based on her retirement goals. Not only did he forget to educate her on risk vs. inflation; but, he didn't find out that her mom was in her late nineties, so this money may have to last thirty years. Wow ... imagine the upside potential that she lost the last few years. Education is so very important when it comes to helping clients see the value of owning different types of **"boats"** so that they may have a chance to succeed. Both of these women were offered something called "plain vanilla investing" and it cost them dearly.

On any given day, in any American city, you can walk into a local specialty ice cream store and look at all the possibilities from vanilla to watermelon, pistachio to cookie dough, and it is heaven! So many flavors— there is something for everyone. Some ice cream shops advertise 50 or more choices, and this is their hook: **CHOICES**. They get you in the door because the variety is so great. It is also a necessity. After all, would you go out of your way, all the way across town even, to buy ice cream if they only had plain vanilla? Of course you wouldn't. You can get plain vanilla anywhere.

Let's apply this same concept to discuss the person who walks into their local bank and asks for retirement advice.

"We have 'vanilla,'" says the man behind the desk.

"Just vanilla?" you ask.

"Yes, we have plain vanilla, vanilla bean, vanilla flavored, and vanilla swirl," says the man.

"So all you have is one option really... **vanilla?**"

"Yes, that is the option," he says.

What a thought – just one option: "vanilla." Now, I do not want to disparage vanilla ice cream at all, vanilla is a sweet pleasure. But is "plain vanilla investing" a pleasure? In the investment world, vanilla is generally defined by a few stock and bond ideas. Usually these ideas are proprietary by nature and worst of all, not what the client needs or truly wants. These are ideas designed by the firm to use with (**all clients and all situations.**) These ideas are force-fed to clients of the firm regardless of unique circumstances. Everyone gets put into the same box without customization. **YOU'RE NOT THE NUMBER ONE PRIORITY!**

The fact is, "plain vanilla" investing just does not have enough options. It reminds me of a quote I once heard, "If you try to act sane in an insane world, you'll get yourself killed." Plain vanilla is a sane way of investing today, which may have worked fine forty years ago, but no longer. We live in a different place and a different time. I don't want to get technical; but derivatives, leverage and computers, along with congressional changes, have made our investment environment insane (**CRAZY!**). It is truly like riding in the ocean through a blinding storm in a sailboat that was designed centuries ago without modern day technology. You're hoping and praying that you'll make it. Today's investment environment is an **insane world!**

To take the concept of "plain vanilla" a bit further, let's compare it with another popular investment term: "buy and hold." Buy and hold is a long term investment strategy based on the view that in the long run financial markets will give a positive rate of return despite periods of volatility or decline. We are assuming the markets are efficient and that the risk reward is correlated. I think that most Americans now realize that this concept is flawed, but they don't know what to do. Can you imagine buying and holding just one company stock for fifty years and not diversifying into other companies? You may have seen the devastation this can cause in your own portfolio, or that of a friend. The next few chapters should help explain why "plain vanilla" and "buy and hold" both need to become things of the past.

Me, Myself, and I

I am a stickler for tradition and it seems appropriate to share a little about myself. I am exceptionally knowledgeable about retirement and investing. I strive to be the best at whatever I do. Even as a child at age fifteen, I decided that I wanted to fly planes. At age seventeen (two years later), I received my pilot's license. After going to college and graduating with a B.A. in Business at U.N.C.C. in 1980, I knew I wanted to start my own corporation, which I did at age 26. After entering this field in the fun decade of the nineties; I knew that I wanted to be the best, so I immediately started to strive for the top designation which in my opinion is: CERTIFIED FINANCIAL PLANNER™ professional or CFP® professional. This designation took almost four years to accomplish; but, the knowledge and education was priceless. Why would anyone want to be average at anything? Strive to be the best! Even so, that doesn't explain why I do what I do, or even why I wrote this book.

Growing up in an Italian family adds a few value statements about a person that are tough to bullet point. Family ties, fellowship over food, and deep-seated, undeniable responsibility are just a few traits that were ingrained in me at such a young age. They shaped me and my future. I am a product of my upbringing. Stereotypical or not, being Italian means a lot of things that are hard to quantify.

On our family farm, my grandparents and uncle were our neighbors. When we had a small get together, thirty family members attended! My family did not know what the word "trivial" meant. I had the joy of being with family in the good times, the comfort of having someone to talk to in the bad times, and the sorrow of seeing the older family members pass away.

The value of nurturing strong relationships was ingrained in me ever since I can remember. I was taught to honor my father and mother, be kind to everyone, and above all; family is the most important thing in your life. Trust and honor were the values that defined a man and "giving your word" was as important—if not more so—than any signed contract. Being trustworthy, honorable, and attainable for the ones you love are just who I am.

I think this is why today I value my client relationships so much. I think of the people with whom I work with, as family. I sincerely enjoy meeting a client at a restaurant and spending the time, (as much time is needed), discussing their family and kids while eating lunch. I see no problem with a call from a client on the weekend to discuss a personal situation. I see this as an extension of how I was raised – to honor and trust, to be trustworthy and to take the time to build relationships. I find that this is valuable two-fold—I get to know what's important to my clients, so that we can make smart investments, and it also gives me the opportunity to build rapport and trust. It is a win-win; and best of all, I get to have notable meals and remarkable conversations with great folks!

When I began to conceive of a book about investing and retirement I knew I didn't want to focus on strategies or risky "one time" get-rich schemes. If you are one of the millions of Americans interested in this kind of investing, there are plenty of late-night infomercials and flashy websites that will happily tell you where and how to put your hard-earned money; and suffice to say, you will probably lose it, if this is the direction you choose.

Looking at things objectively, we have to admit that we are now a society as a whole that requires an easy out. Give us the fast return, a no-work option for our ever-shortening Internet-age attention spans! Not to mention the predators who are out there to take advantage of our insufficiencies and naïve aspirations. So-called "advisors" are sometimes—often times— motivated by their personal greed instead of by the satisfaction of knowing they did right by someone and provided a family a positive financial future. You don't have to watch the news for very long to catch a story on greed and how people were taken advantage of. The past several years have taught us that the people in whom we placed our trust can be very corrupt and insufficient—and that is a scary thought.

Fortunately, for those of you who do see the value in patience, persistence, research, and in relationships, there are a few of us "old-school, new ideas" guys out there. We are passionate about smart investing and providing quality client service. I have been fortunate to have built my business around relationships first. When I work with a client, I make it my job to get to know them, their family, their needs, their wants, their dreams, and their realities. I don't just work with anyone. I can't possibly help every single person achieve the wealth and long-term security they seek. Some people have already made poor decisions that have clouded their future. I would misrepresent myself and my ability if I promised miraculous returns. I would not only be doing that person an injustice, I would be compromising my integrity. I will do neither, and it would be unfair to all of my clients if I tried.

We have established that I can't work with everyone, but after many years of experience, I also know that not everyone can work with me. I am focused, passionate, and deliberate. I demand that my clients are open to a long-term two-way relationship and are as dedicated as I am to their financial stability. I make a lot of phone calls. I like to meet with my clients regularly. The way I see it, all too often, advisors are unwilling to have a personal relationship with their clients. Most advisors seem to want to remain isolated and somehow live above the people they are trying to help.

I also think that it is important to hold my client's accountable for taking "ownership" of their golden years. Have you taken the time to organize, plan, and prepare? At hand are several opportunities to start that process in this book and I encourage the readers to make notes in the margins or on the fill-in sections and take this to your advisors. Thinking about how your life may unfold in the next 30 years may be difficult; nevertheless, there is plenty that you can do today that will assure a more positive outcome.

A trusting and open advisor-client partnership is rare. Yet, one of my philosophies is this: if you're going to trust someone with your savings, with being able to position that savings in such a way that you will have a comfortable life-long income, shouldn't you be able to call them after 5:00 PM if you have questions? Shouldn't you be able to call them on a Saturday if you have an emergency? Shouldn't you have some type of guarantee that you and your family will be able to do the things that you need and want to do? Shouldn't they know that you and your spouse have always wanted to go to Italy?

Here it is: I need honesty, and I demand trust and respect. I don't require that you have a degree in finance, or even care about the minute details. However, I do need you to think about the dreams you envision when it comes to your retirement future. Maintaining your lifestyle is so very important. I work very hard to earn the trust of my clients to help them build and grow our relationship and hopefully, their portfolio. I do this because it matters to me, it's my passion, and it's my life's work.

What makes me unique is that I offer unbiased advice and am not limited to exclusive arrangements. This is important because it allows me to think open-mindedly about the best choice for my clients—to put you first. That is after all what you want, right? And I think that you should have the same service, whomever you choose to work with. It's a complicated conversation describing a relationship of true independence vs. proprietary. I have recently had multiple conversations with proprietary advisors and even they give me the "deer in the headlights" look. They don't understand the independent world. They have lived in an environment of "big company ideology" so long that they're brainwashed. If they could mentally step outside their situation for a day, they would be amazed at the hundreds of possibly better options for their clients. Unfortunately.... I don't believe most will!

Bull vs. Bear Market

Just to simplify, the definition of a Bull market is a prolonged period when stock prices rise faster than the historical average and sentiment is good. A Bear market is when prices are falling and there is widespread pessimism. Both of these are a long term trend and that is what affects the market in such a dramatic way. Do not confuse these large market conditions with short-term market movements.

Beware the Bag of Gold

Do you know how nice it is? Finally this idiot's name (Madoff) is not being brought up every other second of the day! I can now stop explaining the damage that he caused and how he did it. People threw money at him like it was water because of his lies. Risk will always involve the possibility of loss…**there is no free lunch**. A story that sounds too good to be true usually is a lie. I was at the golf course a few years ago and some of the guys were discussing a "money guy" that was promising a double digit growth rate per month by using foreign currency. I just looked at them in passing and said **"BULL."** I think you can guess the rest of the story that finally came out a year later.

I assume that any investment book written today should mention Bernie Madoff. There is always a bad apple in the bunch. I hate the destruction that this one caused. I don't care if you're an attorney, Realtor®, police officer, or judge; terrible people exist in all walks of life. I personally believe that Madoff is mentally ill; he destroyed too many people's lives not to be.

I met with a business owner about ten years ago that was interviewing Financial Professionals. He pulled out one of his account statements, and I was shocked. My five year old son could have drawn this up using excel and a computer. I immediately asked him if he trusted this guy named Madoff. He replied that he was a "big wig" and well known in New York. I replied that I wouldn't trust him. We went our separate ways and all I can do is hope that he pulled his money out early.

Defining Madoff is like clarifying a situation where the fox is in command of the hen house. He had his clients write checks directly to his firm. He controlled the cash and the statements; this is the exception, not the rule. Most Financial Professionals are not allowed to receive monies. Checks are written to the companies where the investments are held. This is a great way to double check your investments because the statements will be sent to you as the investor by these firms. Prudential sends out Prudential Statements and Fidelity sends out Fidelity Statements. Your advisor associate's name will be on the statement as your Financial Professional but the money is held at the institutions.

Milk vs. Mail

So what does milk have to do with mail? Not much ... anymore! If you try to compare your family's weekly gallon of milk with a mail delivery – you get an interesting concept. Years ago when I was growing up, the local milkman would come to the house. (Try telling your child about that today and they'll look at you like you're crazy.) He knew the family, he knew all of the kids by name, and he was available as needed.

Today, the only thing that comes to the house is the mail, and most of it is junk! This goes back to the realization that things have changed—**a lot**. When we think about the "old days," the ideas of a relationship and customer service come to mind. Today, they seem to fall to the wayside all too often.

Our society still values customer service and relationships, yet by the name of "business" and "forward progress." We don't get the friendly relationship-based service that we crave. Service today is the worst that I've ever seen. I tried to call my local cable company last month and was hung up on . . . **TWICE!** I think that it's gotten to the point that we just expect poor service. Heck . . . part of the time that I'm on the phone, I'm not even speaking to someone in the United States. I think we've all experienced that.

Fact of the matter is, if you look at the financial industry today you would be hard pressed to find a Financial Professional willing to come to your home and take the time to get to know you and your family. The average Registered Representative wouldn't even consider it. If you asked him to come to your home—he would reply "Make an appointment - come into the office." Even if you called your family physician, whom you have known for years, he is unlikely to come to you (unless you live in a small town and have some sort of amazing relationship—in which case, lucky you!).

This is what stresses the importance of having an independent advisor associate. The relationship is the most important aspect of investing. You need to know that this advisor is someone you can entrust with your private information, your money, and your dreams. He needs to know you, what your goals are, where your life is at, and how your family is doing. **What is the lifestyle that you expect when you retire?** Once you turn fifty and look at the horizon of retirement, it is important to have someone who is willing to meet you for a cup of coffee, come to the house, and sacrifice a Sunday afternoon if that is what <u>you</u> need. Your finances don't take the day off, and you deserve someone who will put your interests first at all times. You deserve someone that you not only call a friend; but who is also your partner when it comes to your retirement needs.

Investment Philosophy Today

When I sit down with a new client, we talk about possible returns going forward, the risk of both the equity and bond markets, their personal risk analysis, and of course, goals. I hate to think about this past decade and how it was such a roller coaster ride. In the past, we certainly expected to have some up and down years; but that was ridiculous. By their very nature, investments are designed for the long haul and not for the short look. The past decade has shown us the importance of a Financial Professional with competent ideas. I believe that investing is truly an art and not a science. We have no way of knowing what the markets will do over any given period of time. Past performance really doesn't mean anything. It is important to prepare for all scenarios and make sure that you have the correct boats in place for your risk tolerance and goals.

Ironically, when discussing investment software today, some advisors will present client returns that are continuous every single year. Some will show equal returns of 8%, for example, each year without any negative returns. By doing this, short term gains look almost as strong as long term gains. The lack of negative returns will never show the genuine damage that bear markets cause. True returns must look at "the good and the bad", along with their progressions. We now know the damage that negative returns will do to a retirement strategy. History has shown us that the odds are many retirees will live through at least four bear market downturns after they retire. Preparation and a fully customized plan is a must for these market situations.

Let's look at an example. Imagine yourself recently retired with $200,000 in your IRA. You decide that you would like to pull $10,000 out of this account per year. The $10,000 is 5% of the account value. Going forward this money has to stay consistent, generate growth, and hopefully rise with inflation. Maintaining the lifestyle of your dreams is your goal.

Well, guess what? At the end of your first year, the market collapses and you presently have an account that is worth just $150,000. To maintain this $10,000 a year in income, you will now have to withdraw 8%. Watch out, you'll have to receive substantial growth going forward to keep this going. What would you do if this account were to fall to $140k, $130k, $120k, $100k? Now you really have a problem...your hard-earned and carefree retirement is over—and at 66 years old, it is time to go back to work. (**We're not even taking inflation into account!**)

Now some of you may be thinking that you'll get a job and work part time. Maybe you can. What it you can't or your health won't allow it? What will you do and how will your family react? Just something to think about . . .

I saw this unfortunate situation play out a lot from 2000 to 2002 and again 2007 to 2009. Many advisors didn't figure on a bear market rearing its head, and they never adjusted—somehow they expected the market to continue going up steadily, and the fact of the matter is… that just does not happen, especially on a short time horizon. Planning for the worst and hoping for the best is the only way to invest. In the era of the nineties, some accounts were withdrawing as much as 9% with the expectation that their check would never stop. The withdraw percentage amount used today is between three and one half and four percent. **Wow, what a difference**.

Many of the percentage factors used by pensions in the past were way off when it came to life time payouts. This is why many of these plans are currently in trouble. Even after five decent positive years in the market from 2009 to 2015, these plans can't repair their losses due to withdrawal payouts. When you're paying out nine percent and the account is growing at an average of six percent, it's only a matter of time before depletion.

Today, it's very important to realize that many Financial Professionals are still using antiquated game plans, obsolete philosophies, and outmoded software. They are using a flawed system that could force the average retiree of today back to work. That is unacceptable to me, and it should be unacceptable to you too!

I want to emphasize that this book was written for the soon-to-be retiree, not the twenty and thirty year olds. If you have longer than a ten year time horizon, using normal investment tactics can usually maintain some kind of growth even during a bear market, because you have the time to ride it out. But, getting back to even equates to the fact that you've lost both time and the inflation factor. Getting back to the investment amount that you had ten years earlier isn't always an accomplishment.

If, on the other hand, your Financial Professional used a variety of boats to help you tactically avoid loss, your recovery time would be less and your end results should be greater. It's impossible to speculate ahead to see the top and bottom of the markets. Using a multiple of different boats (your fleet) helps to adjust for both quiet and turbulent seas. If you can avoid just half of your potential losses during a major market downswing, think about how much faster your account will grow because of the greater account value once the market turns positive.

What Your Retirement Means

There was once a time when Americans retired in the last few years of their lives only to live off of what meager savings they had accumulated. Many individuals didn't do much or have much—and their health dictated a quiet and slow pace of life. What do you think the current population thinks about retirement?

A vast majority believes that they will never be able to fully retire. They haven't planned correctly or lost too much money in the falling stock market. I don't care about your age … **set a goal!**

For the ones that have planned, it is a time of activity—at least for the first several years. People who are retired choose to go back to school, travel the world, volunteer, and help raise their grandkids. Your retirement can be a time of fulfillment and happiness, activity and energy.

No one knows how long our retirements will last, but anticipating longevity is now a prime factor in investing! You need to plan for 20 years or more for both you AND your spouse. You need to plan for inflation, volatility in the markets, and your needs and wants. Most importantly, you need to have a plan for poor health in your later years so that you and your spouse can have the kind of care you need. Hopefully, your family can accommodate whatever end-of-life care is necessary.

Loss

For those of you that are going through this book without a care or worry . . . wake up. Loss..........true loss, is horrible; especially if it's preventable when it comes to your **retirement.** Do you really want to have to get a job to survive in your seventies?

Webster defines the word **"loss"** as **"destruction or ruin."** If you think about it; whether it be the loss of a baseball game, your favorite watch, your job, or sadly, your spouse...these events are devastating. One of my best friends lost her son last year. "God Forbid" this happen to anyone. I can't even imagine the pain. I'm sure that her agony is every day and a never ending nightmare. I remember waking up many mornings after my Father first passed away thinking that his death . . . **was only a dream** ... quickly realizing . . . he was gone forever.

When we discuss retirement and imagine the pure thought of loss of money, it goes deeper than just an empty **"nest egg."** It gets into areas such as freedom, peace of mind, pride, friendships, family and of course . . . time. Yes . . . we also lose TIME. The time it would take to recapture the loss in the stock market; and as we get older . . . time is of great value.

Most retirees can't afford (nor would they want to) to take major risk in the markets. Time is what allows the younger investors to take this risk. These young kids that are still wearing the "body armor" that most of us lost years ago, haven't lived the pain of major market loss. They haven't seen their cash account fall one hundred thousand dollars overnight; and until they do, they won't know what true market loss is. They have the **time** that retirees wish they had.

Retirement Tax Planning- A Moving Target

For those Americans that believe in our way of life, I salute you! The Constitution seems to have a bull's eye on it and many want to change it. I find it absurd for some to actually believe that our hard saved retirement accounts should be on the chopping block along with the way they are taxed. We'll never be able to know what the future holds for tax planning so I suggest that you strategize for the worst.

I would also suggest that you take advantage of the tax efficient vehicles of today. Current programs such as Roth IRAs, Spousal IRAs, and Stretch IRAs are great ways to save taxes and possibly transfer monies to your heirs very efficiently. If the Government decides to change the Rules midstream, so be it. Hope for the best and find a CFP® professional to help you plan for this moving target . . . taxation.

Ten Questions to Ask an Advisor

Interviewing several Advisor Associates before you decide on whom to choose as your Financial Professional is advisable. In my opinion, I will invariably recommend a CFP® professional that is independent. Be careful...today many Financial Professionals are calling themselves independent. **BULL!** If their Broker Dealer is owned by an insurance or mutual fund company, they are ... **NOT INDEPENDENT!**

Also, I feel it's always best to change Financial Professionals if you feel that you're not given enough attention, if your calls are not returned, or if you're not given full explanations to the usage of your money. If you do not sense that the person you have chosen genuinely cares about your future, find one who will. It is absolutely your right to find the perfect person to guide you through these very difficult decisions.

When you are looking at beginning a long-term investment strategy with the assistance of a Financial Professional, or just seeking a change in advisors, there are a few questions that you should ask upfront. Getting a feel for the type of service and success you will have is very important.

1. Are you a CFP® professional?
2. What investment strategy do you currently have in place in case of an economic or public disaster?
3. What ideas can you show me so that I won't have to worry about waking up at age 70 and looking at a zero balance in my IRA?
4. Are you an Advisor Associate?
5. Are you an independent or captive agent?
6. Do you have a full array of non-proprietary programs?
7. Do you believe in "plain vanilla" investing?
8. What type of alternative investments can you show me?
9. If I have an issue, can I call you personally in the evening or on a Sunday?
10. Will you personally be looking at my account daily?

CHAPTER 3

How Big is Your Fleet?

The world of investing and Retirement Planning has changed forever. The old concepts of "buy and hold," diversification, and asset allocation are not as effective as they were in the past. Stop kidding yourself. Imagine the date is 2015. You're lying in an operating room awaiting major surgery. You're nervous, scared, and unsure of your future. As you look up, you soon realize that you've gone back in time. The doctors, the equipment, and all aspects of this hospital are antiquated. You're thinking to yourself "get me out of here." You understand that medical procedures have come a long way in the past sixty-five years. Past technology is primitive compared to today's standards and you don't want to take the risk using these old concepts. (Maybe you're in a Twilight Zone episode - just kidding; but I think you get the point.)

How do you feel about that? It's the 21st Century and we tend to use investment concepts that were drawn up over fifty years ago. Learning modern conceptual ways of investing and taking advantage of these new ideas may help position you for a successful retirement. Designing a customized fleet of ships so that your retirement doesn't come to an abrupt end is very important. I love the new question: "will you survive the next stock market crash?"

This chapter will discuss the following areas:

- Fundamental Flaws
- Boats: Your Financial Fleet
- Market Loss & Retirement = Oil & Water
- Guarantees

Fundamental Flaws

I know that I may bore some readers with my concepts of fundamental flaws of the investment world. Some individuals just don't get excited about the problems with "plain vanilla!" However, if that sparked your interest, I would like to share a few more concepts about my viewpoint of flawed software.

As I wrote earlier: it is interesting when you take a look at today's Financial Professionals. Some will present, for example, a consistent return of 8% every single year going forward. **NO WAY!** The past decade has shown the absurdity of this thought. Have you ever lived through a ten-year period where the market consistently gained 8% each year? **Certainly not!** The market goes up and the market goes down. Sometimes, the market goes *way* up and *way* down! That is what it does, and to expect otherwise would be naïve.

To be effective, the Financial Professional must show both *substantial downturns and substantial upturns* to achieve real world results. We all have lived through these wild swings, and we need to take them into account when planning our futures. The dramatic effect that a bear market can have on a retirement plan must be shown. Total care must be taken when analyzing bear markets, withdrawals, and inflation during retirement. As I wrote earlier, in the investment world today, many advisors continue to use ideas and tools that are outdated and flawed.

The theory that I have devoted my life to is titled **"Multiple Boat Theory."** It involves the idea of using multiple boats; each working independently and designed for different weather conditions. This is what I have shown my clients for the past decade. To have an effective fleet of investments, there must be a mixture of many dissimilar vessels. These vessels have distinctive tasks and jobs to perform. Your investment and retirement life likens to taking a journey in a ship across treacherous seas. In order for you to survive this journey, why not have many different ships to handle the many different types of weather from calm seas to hurricanes? These boats help take diversification and asset allocation to a new level.

Most investors are traveling in only one large ship; a sail boat, centuries-old, without radar or forecasting equipment. Imagine for a moment: you're on the top deck of this ship in the middle of the ocean. While gazing overboard, you're amazed at the enormous size of the full moon as it glimmers off of the ocean. It takes up half the skylight. Slowly, you feel the temperature drop as the sound of the waves begins to magnify. The winds pick up and very quickly the seas begin to thrust the ship violently. You're forced to go below deck to avoid getting drenched. Within an hour, this ship is in the midst of a large hurricane and lost forever.

It's disturbing, isn't it? The sad truth about this is that many Americans watched their retirement accounts sink just that fast - **TWICE** in the past decade. Many Americans had to put their retirement on the back burner and some have yet to retire. Having to work as older adults is a complete struggle and those that haven't planned are truly in trouble.

Boats: Your Financial Fleet

This section involves customizing your fleet, choosing your boats and your game plan. The process of setting up this arch for protection and growth to help stabilize your retirement future is very important. Your family must be able to weather any type of storm. Each plan is specialized based on risk and longevity. If your wife's parents are in their late nineties and you both wish to retire at sixty … you better have a plan. This fleet needs to take into account social security (and what is the most efficient ages to take it) along with the many boat options today. Investing in only bonds when you should have a large portion in equities to fight inflation, could be a disaster. This plan should be individualized because every family is different.

Boats come in all sizes, all speeds, and all types. A sail boat can turn a weekend into a gloriously enjoyable experience. A shiny new speedboat can race through the waves, get your adrenaline going, and get you to your destination quickly. I use the boat analogy to describe my investment philosophy because I feel it best describes how you may want to think of your investments—as many options and opportunities, depending on conditions and the situation at the time. If you can take a sailboat—it is a lovely way to travel if you need to get there without worrying about weather. If a storm is coming—take the sub. While most advisors will discuss the importance of diversification between stocks, bonds, and cash, I take that concept to the next level. Yes, you need to diversify, but I don't just believe you should spread out your investment capital. I believe you need to *strategically* locate your investment money in order to get the best return and hopefully avoid the danger.

Now, don't lose me. I believe that the investment world of open-end funds, closed-end funds, emerging markets, hedged equity, technology focused equity, sector positions, public/private equity, small company, mid company, large company, leveraged investments, inverse investments, international investments, managed futures, long/short positions, bond positions, direct participation programs, real estate investment trusts, limited partnerships, general partnerships, and cash may all be used for a multiple of different seas. Some will be better for calm weather and others better for hurricanes. Some will not be affected by the basic market movement and others will move drastically. Your fleet must be versatile and able to change quickly. This concept is very confusing, and I would suggest that you discuss it with a Financial Professional. These investments are not suitable for everyone.

Other types of investments should be used to handle calm seas, rough seas, and hurricanes as well. Some investment options may be more appropriate because many of them are less affected by the stock market movement—and this can protect you from wild swings. These investments can also help you to sleep better at night because they can be tied to guaranteeing lifetime income even in major market downturns. It really depends on how you feel about risk and what your family thinks about...
peace of mind!

Today's environment is getting very tricky. Many investments are moving in identical directions, thus making true diversification very difficult to predict. Using my theory will help to solve this dilemma.

Sail Boat: A sail boat can be a lovely way to get from point A to point B. It is the perfect vehicle when you have all day to get to shore. Fairly reliable, a sailboat may not be quick (unless a good gust of wind hits the sail—which happens); but with today's modern sailboats, you will get there, and you will be safe and comfortable. Some days you will catch a good breeze, others you may stall out in the middle of the lake. Now, most investors are in a sailboat that is centuries old! This one ancient boat is their entire portfolio. The old boat moves along slowly hoping the wind will pull it toward its destination; however, not able to see possible troubled storms ahead.

Our new sailboat is <u>different</u>; it is a modern day beauty with all the technology and radar equipment needed. It is faster because it can read the wind from afar and safer because it can avoid a storm. This is just one of our boats, and it tends to follow a fundamental approach to stay invested in the correct areas, but watch for trouble so it can be avoided.

Submarine: The submarine is a stealth vehicle, staying well below water at a constant speed and actually riding under any large storm, to reach its destination. A submarine can keep moving forward under the radar to avoid any turbulence in the seas of the market. You may not have to worry about wind or rain in a sub because conditions don't affect this powerful nuclear vessel. Don't expect a quick or glamorous ride, but the sub may get you there "steady as she goes."

Speedboat: Brisk, quick, and speedy; what a ride! The speedboat is a super-quick and risky ride, but it is a fun one. The speedboat is certainly a thrill … that is, unless you hit a bad wake or cut a turn too soon. The risk may be worth the reward for the speed of this vehicle, but watch out because with the reward, it may also bring danger. This speedboat is very fast and some investors that can handle the risk and need the added possible returns may want the ride. Using a small portion of your portfolio as a speed boat may help to gain significant returns when the waters are calm. I do think that if you feel a speedboat is a ride you find interesting, you may want to guarantee it…I'll discuss this later.

Aircraft Carrier: The aircraft carrier can make the long haul. Equipped with speedy craft of its own, the aircraft carrier is a powerhouse, moving swiftly and surely but not setting any land-speed records. The carrier is designed to set aircraft to flight and help them reach their destination. These aircraft have different speeds of their own and maintain a steady flow of movement. They also have aircraft that can reach a destination easier because of purpose and location. These aircraft can act as dividends and possibly pay out a steady flow of income at any time.

Market Loss & Retirement = Oil & Water

Many of us aspire to a happy retirement starting at age 60 or earlier. With this, comes the real possibility of either spouse living until age 90, and those thirty years of life will have their own distinct "phases." Whether you agree that this is a possibility for you or not; many Americans will see this reality because of advances in medicine and heredity.

Years ago, when I attended a long term care conference, they discussed the three phases of retirement: **"Go Go," "Slow Go,"** and **"No Go."** This was interesting to note because many of my clients in their fifties and sixties realize the fact that one day, they will not have the stamina or the health to always be on the move. Our goal is to stay healthy and attempt to enjoy retirement; while being cautious about what is yet to come. Our health costs can get expensive as we age and the worst thing that can happen as we go into our retirement is a significant market loss that threatens our ability to take care of these needs.

A portfolio loss, plus retirement, is the same as oil and water; they don't mix. Let's go over the example from Chapter 1. A theoretical $100,000 IRA account that experiences a 33% market loss will bring the balance to $67,000. Most would look at this and assume that a 33% account gain would get this account back to even; but just look: $67,000 x 1.33% = $89,110 not the $100,000 we started with. Beware of double digit loses in retirement.

Let's go one step further: if a retiree is taking a 6% withdrawal along with this earlier market loss, the total number after the market downturn, is approximately $61,000 after the first year. Wow! Now this person would have to receive a market appreciation of approximately 65%. Most readers are way ahead of this statement realizing that this is still an issue because the client is still pulling $6,000 out of the account yearly. Remarkably we need approximately a 75% return the second year. What a problem!

I know, "wait a minute." Some of you are recalling from Chapter 1; "What about inflation?" Inflation is the silent killer that many don't realize truly exists. If we guess an inflation number of a mere 3% per year, we now need a return of approximately 100% in the second year, to get back to even. The moral of the story tells us: when a bear market strikes a retirement plan that is withdrawing money consistently each year and planning for inflation, this causes a **"perfect storm."** This plan now has a slim chance of survival. This is especially important within that five year window before and after retirement begins. Market loss and retirement is like oil and water, they don't mix!

Diversification is an interesting concept to re-introduce at this juncture because it can do two things: 1) guard against loss and 2) guard against gain. What a dilemma. If your advisor has allocated your account correctly; nevertheless, we have a devastating drop and your account loses 33%, the chances are slim through diversification that you will reach your goal unless you have a lot of time. Diversification is a true double edged sword, lower loss and lower return......**This is a conundrum!**

Guarantees
To guarantee or not to guarantee... That is the question

In this new edition, I have decided to keep this section to a minimum. I believe you need to find a CFP® professional to help you through this arena of ideas. These products are extremely complex, but I believe necessary.

Let's get to the fun stuff: Guarantees. To some, "guarantees" are a scary word; we tend to think about the cost and not the value. However, we all love when our flat screen TV, car, or computer has a warranty. My Big Screen television broke back in 2009 and it was replaced with the Mack-Daddy new model ... I loved it! No money out of my pocket. Sure, I paid over $500 for the extra 4 years of warranty coverage, but guess what? I received the equivalent of an $8,000 TV for that cost. (It's amazing how the price of a new television or computer has lowered.)

Who do we blame when a product breaks? Do we blame the TV manufacturer, the repair guy, the company that designs the mother board, or me, the movie lover? I don't know. I hope the company that designed the TV was doing the best that they could do; but guess what..."crap happens." Have you ever thought about guaranteeing your retirement income? What if you didn't have to worry about receiving that retirement check each month, especially if the market crashed? The money would be there for you, no matter what the stock market was doing. Then again, if your representative was doing his best, choosing good managers, picking the best funds, and for no fault of his own ... the market crashed ... who do you blame? Have you ever thought about guaranteeing a portion of your retirement income? **I Have!**

When I write about guarantees, I would like you to think back to what I wrote earlier when it comes to the various boats ... especially the **sailboat and speedboat.** Guarantees in life make sense when you receive true value. Why wouldn't you guarantee against income loss in retirement? A hurricane could appear at any time and wreck a sailboat; while a slight gust of wind could destroy a speed boat. Some of you are thinking "I'll just invest in bonds and I don't have to guarantee anything." Wait a minute ... as we discussed earlier: first of all, bonds usually won't give inflation coverage; second, bonds may also lose money - possibly a lot of money. Many Americans may need a variety of boats to achieve income and growth through retirement. The crazy thing about today is that interest rates are so low that the bond market is possibly more risky that the equity market. Many conservative investors may one day open their statements to see a substantial loss in their accounts and wonder why.

When designing a program of boats that may help supply income for the rest of your life, the boat selection is very important. Americans may have a mixture of different types of vehicles from which to pull income. Social Security is probably the foundation for most, and for the lucky one's, maybe a pension. After that, a variety of different boats may supply the excess need. Don't forget that you are trying to design a fleet that will hopefully help you live up to thirty years without having to make a paycheck. Who wants to go back to work in their late seventies? I don't. You must plan for this "second half of life."

You will need a full assortment of boats comprising of many variables... liquidity, safety, income, possible growth, and guarantees. Growth potential involves risk and risk involves loss. We know the market downturns are going to happen and their dramatic effect to a retiree may be catastrophic. Retirement is all about income and the planning of retirement is all about that expected monthly check. It needs to be consistent and long-lasting. The goal is to peel the "onion" without destroying its essence; this "onion" needs to last your lifetime.

A four letter word, "annuity" (ok, ok, not technically a four letter word but you get the point), may be useful to some when it comes to income, growth potential, and guarantees. An annuity is a life insurance contract between you and an insurance company. It involves payments for a specific time period or your lifetime. These guarantees are backed by the insurance company. Please, open your mind and put the cost to the side for a moment...let's look at value.

I think all of us have heard the radio and television "talking heads" discuss these products. Usually they discuss the fees or negative side without truly getting into the positive upside potential of how they work. I suggest that you find a CFP® professional that is fully licensed to show you the multiple options and explain how each boat works. You need to look at all of these products . . . not just the basic ones. Make your own opinion after discussing the options. Don't let these "talking heads" of TV and Radio decide for you.

Statistics show that the average bear market comes along every five to six years. Most Americans would like to plan for an uneventful retirement of twenty five years plus. Can they survive a bear market during retirement? Especially in the early years – Can they survive several? The answer is usually **No.** If you retire at 60 and live until age 85, in order to survive a 33% loss in the market, you will need to have almost a 100% profit to catch up. A normal investor believes that a 33% loss needs a 33% gain, and as we discussed earlier, this is just not true. You always have to factor in inflation, income, and you may want to be diversified.

Here is a scenario: You finally retire at 65, you have $200,000 in a brokerage account and start withdrawing $10,000 a year to live. At age 70, you open your statement and are shocked to see your balance has fallen to $100,000. In a panic you realize that your money will be depleted within the decade. What will you do? For most, this means running scared and going entirely into bonds or cash to truly seal their fate. If you had purchased the correct annuity at 65, that monthly check may have kept coming. This would have possibly allowed you to stay in equities, to at least give you a chance to grow your account. After all, *what if you live?*

Most investors do not realize that aligning their money into a total bond or cash posture, may lock in current income, but seal a minuscule growth potential, allowing inflation to slowly draw down the reserves. Odds are; if you are 100% in cash, you will open your statement at some date in the future and see a zero balance. A diversified equity position allows a larger possibility for growth, which more retirees need. This will be discussed further in later chapters.

The bottom line: Many Americans will need some type of guarantee with their investments if they want to avoid the pain of waking up at age 75 broke and looking for work. Many of the boats that I talk about may need guarantees, because fighting inflation along the way by investing in equities and alternatives is a must for most Americans. These products are complicated, and won't work for everyone … talk to your representative for the best custom solution for you and your family. Read the prospectus and look at the differences. This is where having a good solid relationship with your CFP® professional is paramount.

CHAPTER 4

The Dilemma of Aging:
Prepare, find your passion and your faith

Can you imagine going back hundreds of years and living in an era where the life expectancy was just 30-40 years? You would wake up as a teenager and realize that your life is half over ... what a depressing thought! You would be middle age by age 15!

Earlier in the 20th century, when many of our grandparents were born, the life expectancy was 40 years old. Unsatisfactory medical services along with untreatable illnesses were major concerns. These issues crippled and killed many people. Those who survived into adulthood often saw their children and grandchildren die before them because of miserable healthcare and lack of knowledge. So many died of chronic and acute conditions in that era; whereas today, we would just swallow a pill!

This chapter will discuss the following areas:

- Life Stages
- How Old is Old?
- Employment and Old Age
- Crime and Old Age
- Fear of Change
- Keep the Faith
- Family Today
- Things to Consider About Later Retirement
- Long Term Care
- Strategies for the Final Days

Life Stages

Today we are truly living longer and seeing life-related issues that are very concerning. All of our life stages can be very rewarding if strategies are put into place to be able to enjoy them to the fullest. Every living being must have a passion to survive and a will and need to find it. As we get older, this passion may change, but it must be found in order to live every stage of life to its fullest.

If we look at the retirement stages of life and assume that middle age is the "**Go-Go**" Phase, retirement age is the "**Slow-Go**" Phase, and old age is the "**No-Go**" Phase. That sort-of says it all, but I want to make a declaration that you, the readers, must always remember: "you are only as old as you feel." The topic of aging can be one of excitement and new experiences, or it can be one that many find depressing. These stages are just numbers, and I hope that most of you will feel 40 at 70, live life to the fullest, and seek your passion. Eat right, workout often, see your doctor, and tell the rest of the naysayers to **"go to hell"** whenever possible. Age is just a number and life is what you make of it …

The so called "middle age" is a time when we start realizing that our bodies are changing (again!). Physically, we start to see that we are on the downhill side of the mountain. Things that we once did with ease become more difficult and our bodies don't heal as fast. Vision and hearing start to change, and emotionally we begin to take on more challenging activities to fight the fight. For me personally, I received my pilot's license as a teenager and was surprised to know that my vision at that early age was 20/10. In my late forties my eyesight began to change, but luckily, I still don't wear glasses. I will soon "see" a day where glasses or surgery are my reality. My largest complaint is reading books and articles … **my arms aren't long enough!**

On the other hand, my hearing started changing in my fifties. Be it a sign of my age or not; I can tell you this bothers me. I can be in a large room and hear more background noise than the person 2 feet away from me. I really have to listen well to catch all the words. It's exhausting and it makes me "feel" old. One of my clients went to a specialist last week and was told that most men wait seven years too long to get help. I believe that!

Another client was telling me about his own hearing issues. He said that his ears only hear certain tones; so as the person is speaking to him, his brain may interpret the words totally wrong. Now, let me explain that he found this funny; but I think it would drive me crazy, not to mention cause a lot of problems. Aging is not always fun; but it is a good excuse for not hearing your wife when she asks you to take out the garbage!

Now on the other hand, socially, middle age is a time when we tend to have higher paying jobs and higher family satisfaction. It is a great time of life when we start to see our lives in a different way. Many people in their "middle age" spend significant time trying to be a better person for their kids, grandkids, and parents. Many 40 and 50-year-olds are in leadership positions in corporations or are the owners of their own companies. At this age, we also have positions where respect from our peers at the office is a given—we are old enough to be respected, and young enough to have the energy to make changes. This is a great time; however, this is also where we later can see a problem when we start defining our value as our job and not our intrinsic human value: You ARE a doctor, you ARE a teacher.

The stage of "later adulthood" or "retirement," comes into play sometime in our mid sixties. This is the stage that most of us quit work and make significant changes in our lives. The **"Slow-Go"** Phase is a phase of fun and caution. Travel and enjoy life to its fullest because this phase can change abruptly. A fall or sudden scare can change our motivation. Death seems to be all around us when this stage hits us, as we see many of our friends and family get sick and pass away. Physical activities become harder and more difficult to maintain, and depression can creep up on us. Unless we are very structured and driven, we tend to slow down and some just give up the physical workout battle.

My mother, Ruth Gargano is extraordinary. She has maintained a workout for many years through retirement and is now in her early eighties. I truly believe that some days she is a person that would pass for someone in her mid sixties. Unfortunately, this is not the case for everyone. Lately, she herself is starting to slow down. It's very sad … if God gives us the chance to live long enough … we'll all see the **"No-Go"** Phase. I love her dearly and I see that she is getting close to this later phase of life.

I want to touch on the retirement issues that may arise during this stage of "later adulthood." Look for passion in everything you enjoy. My Father was one of the most passionate individuals that I've ever known. He could sit and have a discussion with a stranger to talk about how wonderful life was. There is passion in every facet of life. The key is to keep a positive attitude at all times. Mentally, you will go through many high and low periods, try to find good friends that care about you and have the same concerns.

Stages are just that … stages; and until the end, they keep on coming. It is important that no matter what stage you are in today; make it the best it can be. Remember that preparing for it mentally AND financially will make it all that much better.

How Old is Old?

"Old age" is a stage that many fear the most. It usually comes about in your late seventies, but some are fortunate to delay this with good health into their 80's or 90's. Traditionally, "old age" is categorized by frailty and mental loss. I think we know an older individual that can barely walk, who needs a cane or a walker to get around—who is "old." One of my friends was telling me just last week that her mother had such a poor hip that she must be carried or wheeled everywhere. Mentally she is fine, but physically she is 100% dependent on her family. My heart breaks to think of how a once vital and healthy person, one with full mental capacities, could go to a place where they need to be carried like a child.

Old age is a time where dementia, disabling diseases, activity loss, dependency, Alzheimer's, and death are brought to the forefront. I had a personal experience some twenty years ago that illustrates how this can affect not only the individual, but the whole family.

My Uncle Roy drove into my hometown of Charlotte, North Carolina and became completely disoriented. I need to preface this by writing that he had come to town many times in prior years. We knew something was wrong and soon after that episode, he went into full blown Alzheimer's. During that period of time, it was amazing the way he remembered his childhood. One day, my mother and he drove out to their family farm where they both grew up in Michigan. She was fascinated by the experiences that he remembered. It was like it was yesterday for him. On the other hand, he didn't recognize anyone in the present time; his children and grandchildren were strangers, and his grasp on the activities of the day was sporadic. He died five years later.

Old age, (and I mean that to be the time in your life when you are truly "old," despite your chronological age), is definitely the bottom of the mountain and a destination of finality. I remember a quote from one of those Arnold Schwarzenegger "Conan" movies, where his girlfriend asked **"do you want to live forever?"** I think that if all of us could pick a peak time in our lives before our down fall of dignity, we may choose that as a great time to leave this world. No one wants to live without dignity and being a dependent and helpless creature is a life that lacks honor. As I have said… being "old" is no fun.

I had a great meeting with one of my favorite clients last year. I sat with both her and her parents for lunch. We had a conversation about how many older individuals are living into their nineties and how they were looking forward to this lifespan. I was alarmed when her parents both looked at me and started laughing at the same time. I slowly asked why they were laughing. They smiled and gently said **"no way."** They had already seen health issues and did not want to live a life of miserable health and lacking dignity. It was eye opening. They had decided not to live to be "old." They would choose other options—of which we can only assume. I did not ask!

How old is old? Well, that is hard to quantify—it is probably different for everyone. I have known 90 year olds that were not "old" and 40 year olds that were. There are websites one can go to today that will tell you your "true age," or chronological age, versus your functional age. What age are you "functioning" at? Can you imagine a professional football player and the functioning age of his knees in his 50's? If he maintains his original knees he may have the knees of a ninety year old. I watched a television special showing the work out of a seasoned professional football player in his later years in 2009. He truly couldn't even practice during the week because of the knee swelling and pain. It made me hurt watching the show. Even as an athlete, this man had parts of his body that functioned as if he were 100 years old. Talk about the phrase, "you are only as old as you feel." In reality: this man functioned as a cripple six days a week, as an injured 38 year old four hours a week, and as an accident victim directly after each game. Can you image how this man will spend his "middle age?"

On the other hand; can you imagine a non-smoking woman that maintains good mental health, good physical health, and swims daily, and takes notable care of herself through her 50s? Her functional age may be 35 … how remarkable is that? A great workout, low stress, healthy eating habit, and a good attitude can do wonders. How old you are, at least in some cases, is something you can control—and my recommendation is that you do what you need to do to keep your age in your control for as long as you can!

Truth is, being healthy—as healthy as you can be, is going to make living off your retirement investments a whole lot easier. Being sick, frail, and dependant is expensive. The best retirement investment you can make will be in yourself!

Employment and Old Age

I am currently in a BNI (business networking) group in Charlotte, North Carolina. I own my business and maintain relationships with many younger adults. In my late 50's, I am just beginning to see the animosity towards older adults that exists in some of the 20 and 30 year olds. Maybe it is because they did not benefit from growing up watching the great television actors such as Jimmy Stewart or John Wayne. Perhaps it is my generation's fault for not instilling the values of respect and good judgment.

Older mentors have helped many athletes and professional individuals. I guess the 80/20 rule comes into effect. Twenty percent of the people may truly improve because they are willing to listen and benefit from other's mistakes. Eighty percent will never get it. People like me must take the time and effort to help these young individuals find the tools they need to take care of themselves. Younger generations may not have the skill sets today; but it is not entirely their fault … we did this to them, and hopefully there is time to change it.

I have always been a person that was willing to learn from the experienced individual—no matter what their age. I think many of us realize that experience is far greater than book-smart knowledge. Age discrimination and the work force is a not only unlawful but poor practice; however, it does happen. Businesses may want a younger-looking employee; or they downsize and fire the thirty-year employee that is 55 years old and making $100,000 a year to hire the 25 year old and pay him $30,000 for the same job. My studies show that today nearly 20% of men in the workforce are 65 or older, where in the earlier part of the last century it was roughly 60%. But, things are changing. It's sad that currently Obamacare is destroying the way companies hire and offer benefits to their employees. We are becoming a nation of part-timers. It's sad, today we are leading the world with jobs created at fast food restaurants. *How ridiculous is that?* Hopefully our nation will eventually wakeup and see the light.

I remember when I worked for my old firm in the nineties. They came in and cleaned house when it came to the older doctors and managers upstairs. These were experienced people that were making a good check in the life insurance and estate planning departments. They were replaced by some young "newbies." At that time, I was working on an estate case where one of my best clients needed an additional $400,000 of life insurance. He applied but never gave a check while he was waiting for approval.

The rules of life insurance involve the fact that until a check is received by the company; the client is not insured because they have not given consideration. Even if you are approved, until consideration is received, you're not covered.

I received a call one morning after I had left a message on his office phone, that he had been approved. His wife called in a frantic state to tell me that he was in the hospital with a brain tumor and was going into surgery. I promptly went to my boss and asked if I should deliver my client's approved insurance policy, get it signed before the operation, and collect the check. He called upstairs and talked to the new management and was told it was okay. Now, I am a "black and white" kind of guy when it comes to the rules; so I immediately said "what?" I thought that this would have traditionally been a game-changer.

Let me explain to you that I asked repeatedly if this was OK. After all, the man had a brain tumor; had not given us any consideration, and was possibly terminal. I truly cared about my client and his family; but I had to follow the rules. After going through eight people upstairs, I was told to collect the check.

I went to the hospital, picked up the check, and had him sign the form. He was covered and consideration was received.

Needless to say, I was called into the office three days later and jumped on for delivering a life insurance policy to a dying man. I'll never forget it; I walked into my boss's office and saw 6 "suits" sitting there. I was asked if the check was received and asked to leave the office. The next day my boss walked into my office to ask why I ever got him involved in this.

I replied, "Because it's your job."

Unfortunately, 6 months later my client died; but at least his wife received an additional $400,000 check. And this was all done because the company terminated some older, more experienced managers who would never have let that go through. I don't know what they saved that year by downsizing; but, I doubt it was more than $400,000.

An older, more experienced manager would have known not to grant this insurance, and the company paid for it. At least in this case, karma won out – but that may hardly be a consolation to the many experienced (older) people who lost their jobs.

Crime and Old Age

Crime against older Americans is on the rise. Elder abuse, assault, identity theft, and other horrific crimes are all unfortunate reminders of today's hostility. I remember a movie with James Caan and John Wayne named, *"Eldorado."* James played an inexperienced character that couldn't shoot well so he had to purchase a sawed-off-shotgun type of a pistol. Think of your average 70 year old "packing heat." It is probably a necessity if a fight is coming and a shotgun sounds good to me!

Crime waves are also the reason why these senior communities are popping up. Guarded-gate and age requirements are becoming more popular so that seniors feel that they are safer from the brutality of today's world. It is common sense that most 70-year-olds can't fight a 30-year-old. Not only is physical strength an issue, but the older person has to fear that they may never recover from the injuries. Injuries of any kind are to be avoided at any cost during our old age phase—we just can't heal as fast, or as well.

Fear of Change

The concept "fear of change" has many stages when we are discussing aging. The first step is "denial," or rejecting the concept, and the planning required to think strategically about their future. I think denial happens many times in life whether it be changing your golf swing or changing a tooth brush. Identifying oneself as someone who is getting older is the first step towards preparing for the future. We must face the future, find our passions, and figure out who we are in the next phase of life.

The second step in aging is the "possibility stage;" the stage where we start slowly thinking about the facts of our current situation. Everyone has certain motivations that will either slow or progress them through this phase. Some will come to this phase faster than others. I believe that the thriving and active will accept this stage sooner and enjoy it more—everything is easier when you are sound. This "what if" kind of mentality will bring the individual to the "acceptance phase."

The "acceptance phase" is where the individual can see their hopes, dreams, and true meaning of life come to fruition. We have all seen family members go through illness, dementia, Alzheimer's, frailty, or death. The fear of any or all of these can motivate many individuals in different ways. The ironic truth about fear is that once accepted, it will motivate more than pleasure. If we plan ahead, we can maintain control of our life.

Some experts may analyze these aspects of life and find many more stages. For me, these were the basics. I am not afraid to tell you that my personal fear has always been the fear of being "broke" and "poor" at the same time. One is a fact of life and the other is your perception of it. I don't want to be one of those individuals on the side of the road in the beat-up twenty year old car as smoke billows from the engine. I don't know about your fears; but avoiding a situation of true desolation or dependency is pain for me, and a reason to act. It is important to define your dreams and passions as we get older. Find out what is truly significant and strive toward it. **Open your eyes and plan!**

Keep the Faith

What is the old saying? "Faith can move mountains." Keeping the faith is an area where one must face the realities of life's completion and look towards a finality of hope. Some readers may express their opinion that this section has nothing to do with retirement or aging. I disagree. Every individual in this world has meaning and purpose in life. As we near the end, faith will not only help us to maintain our strength, it will also help us to keep **"our eyes on the ball"** longer. By doing this, our passions may thrive, and our purpose be fulfilled.

I know that the range of my readers will be broad from total agnostic to someone like my grandmother, Mini Gargano. She prayed daily and devotedly followed God's Word. One must decide where their place is when it comes to the meaning of life and their own life story, and how faith and religion fit into it. Individuals, families, and civilizations have moved toward religion when a dramatic change was becoming more prevalent. We are possibly there today.

Now, I look at myself as a closet religious person because everyone has their own individuality and beliefs. I won't push; but if you ask, I will tell you my thoughts and experiences. I sometimes laugh at myself. There was a time when I would have been quiet when it came to politics and religion. Today, don't ask if you don't want my opinion! I am at the time in my life that I will express my total thoughts, while holding nothing back. I believe in total honesty.

I have personally experienced many episodes that prove to me that God exists. For those that don't know or question this experience for themselves, I feel sorrow. It is almost like buying a car. Once you decide the make and model, as you drive around town, you see that car everywhere and don't know why so many people have your same taste.

There are an abundance of many small miracles if you would just open your eyes. Before my Father died, I had been looking for my favorite suit. I couldn't find it anywhere. The day of the funeral, I opened my closet and my suit was directly in the center. It wasn't there earlier that day...I had looked. I almost drowned as a young boy in Lake Michigan...as I was going under for the third and last time, my feet found ground...(the ironic thing about my possible death was that as I was struggling, I could see the adults on shore and no one was paying attention to my possible fate). Recently, a mother and baby went off the road and into a river in Utah. The car was upside down and partially submerged in water. As the emergency team came toward the automobile they all heard a women's voice asking for help. They righted the car and pulled the baby out from the backseat. She was alive. As they approached the mother in the front of the car, they halted suddenly...they could see that she had been dead for hours. The baby was saved, but who's voice did they hear? Seek and you will find.

I believe as we get older our individuality becomes more prevalent. The reserved become more shy, as the resounding and dramatic become more serious. Faith may help many find meaning for their existence and a peace of mind. In some cases, religion will help guide you through the process of aging. If you find yourself in the position to open up towards the ideas of faith, I believe you will find great satisfaction in doing so. If you choose not to embrace faith, may I recommend you consider learning about the history and customs of various religions? It is remarkable to see why dissimilar people believe what they do. Human beings have such a rich and interesting existence on this Earth. The study of how different cultures and religions celebrate life, death, and the afterlife, is at the very least, fascinating!

No matter where you stand on God, religion, and faith, it is important to explore this as you look towards your retirement and the end of your life. You may find that many of your decisions are made more easily when looking at it through this perspective. What is the old saying? **"None of us are going to get out of here alive!"**

Family Today

Having a family supported by both parents is important. This is the foundation for the American way of life and I was blessed with a large Italian family as a child. I am a third generation Italian and I truly love this country. I had the opportunity to watch my nephew graduate from boot camp at Fort Jackson in South Carolina, a few years ago. It's hard to explain my personal emotion that I felt that day … I was so excited and proud. The pride that we feel for our child, our country, or a great friend is truly a gift from God. It's an emotion that we feel; and they themselves see on our face because we can't hide it. Pride is one of those emotions that we can't put a price on (nor would we).

My father always expressed his love and pride for our family and this country along with his words "family is the only thing you can count on in this world and we live in the greatest country in the world today." I was told stories of how my grandfather risked his life to come over on a ship as a young man because of the opportunities in America. He worked on the railroad until he could save enough money to buy his farm in Benton Harbor, Michigan. The respect and love I give my father, grandfather, and our country is rare today.

Television in the late fifties and early sixties was fun as a child (granted we only had five or six channels to watch). I'll never forget watching John Wayne, Gregory Peck, Jimmy Stewart, Burt Lancaster, and the many hero actors in those westerns and war movies. They helped build a structure of strength and loyalty for our way of life for most kids. I think it's funny the way that we felt Western Movies would be popular forever. Kids today find them boring and slow. Society is changing … I hope for the better!

Do any of you remember the *old* series "The Adventures of Superman" with George Reeves? Part of their promotion for the beginning of the series uttered these words: "He fights a never ending battle for truth, justice, and the American Way." Man, are those great words or what? Does anyone talk about America that way any more? Wow … I wonder why. Actually I don't wonder why!!!! If you're reading this book and you truly care about our country and our way of life … **you better wake up.**

It's sad today to realize the agenda of politics and how the masses of Americans are not paying attention. My eleventh grade history teacher was awesome. His favorite quote was "the masses are asses." (So true today.) He always expressed the fact that most are clueless when it comes to politics and would rather live with their head in the sand than really know the truth of the world. The foundation of every American starts with the home. The respect we learn for our parents and God, along with a strong family structure, is ingrained in us forever. If this is not present....the child is lost.

Things to Consider About Later Retirement

There are many things to consider when thinking about retirement and I see things mostly from an investment perspective; so I took the time to sit with Ernie Linger, who was the Manager at Carmel Place retirement home in Charlotte, North Carolina. He discussed a few main issues when it comes to retirement home living involving monetary and emotional concerns. These concerns may also apply to retirees who live on their own.

Being Too Healthy: In many cases, older retirees actually plan on dying years earlier. Ernie said that many of the residents in his community were outliving their money and depending on Social Security 100% for their living expenses. They had never dreamed that they would live this long.

Social Security Doesn't Cut It: Retirement homes and other care facilities must raise rates to survive. Cost of living has gone up even though the government says it hasn't. Social Security will not cover all of the basic costs of being retired today. For many, this is all they have.

Retirees Suffer From "The Mom" Syndrome: Many retirees feel that they must help their children no matter what. They never stop looking out for their kids, even the ones who left the house 40 years ago! Some children are out of work, some need money for the grandchildren, and some just want a handout. All of this generosity from the parents is causing them significant hardship.

Family Abandonment: It is a traumatizing situation when the children live in town but never see their Mom or Grandmother. Children get busy and life tends to get in the way, but that is little consolation for an older retiree who is alone. Ernie said that very few children and grandchildren ever come by and take their mother out for a drive or to a grandchild's ballgame. This is very sad.

Medicare Doesn't Cut It: Prescription drugs, eyeglasses, hearing aids, and dental health care can all suffer, when retirees rely on just Medicare. Many let their bodies go because of expense issues and their quality of life can suffer greatly. Ernie told me of a case where a woman didn't get a new hearing aid and kept missing breakfast, lunch, or dinner because she didn't hear the bell. Obamacare is draining substantial monies from Medicare; so make sure to plan with your doctor for these changes. When planning your retirement, make sure to budget for general supplemental health care insurance. Even this can be a substantial amount of dollars if you are facing the scenario: **What if you live?**

I thought these issues were very interesting and would like you to carefully consider what Ernie has observed in his many years of working with the residents of Carmel Place. Fortunately, there are people like him and places like that, which look out for us if we need or want to transition to a retirement home.

Long Term Care

Long Term Care, Medicare and Medicaid are confusing; but I would be remiss as a retirement planner not to address Long Term Care Insurance. If you're rich enough, that you can spend and don't care; then you possibly don't need it. If you're poor enough that a minor stay in the hospital will totally wipe out your savings, then you possibly can't afford it. If you're somewhere in the middle, you probably need it and can afford it. Go ahead and check on pricing, benefits, and find someone you can trust to help you avoid the pain of dependency and burden.

A sad fact is that in the last years of our lives, we sometimes spend many days, even months, hospitalized. This is expensive and not a pleasant way to leave this world; but it is many times the reality. Making the decisions about how your family is supposed to deal with this situation ahead of time is a gift. As much as providing for the best caregivers and facility; making your wishes clear will be a great assistance to your children and grandchildren. Take the time now to make those important choices. Prepare for the worst and hope for the best.

Strategies for the Final Days

Strategizing about the medical nature of the final days is a combination of accepting the brutal facts and preparing for your future. This book discusses investment and retirement planning; but ultimately, it is about planning and preparation.

This book emphasizes living and it's not necessarily about your death; but I do want to make a comment on your children's inheritance. Your children may expect an inheritance and if this is part of your plan … great. The largest gift that you can give them is to put together a "full proof" retirement plan and prepare for your future. You personally don't want to become a burden on them in your later life by either needing money or care. Leaving this world with dignity is so very important.

Your children may not want to admit this because they love you, but changing a parent's diapers is not really on their agenda. I do want to bullet point some questions you may want to bring to an Estate Planning Attorney and CFP® professional.

This is your homework: Answer the following questions. Write out the answer, and any notes, such as the name of your planner and attorney. Share this information with your loved ones and make sure to put it in a safe place in case of an emergency, so that your family can take care of any issues they need to. If any of the questions reveal that you need to make a change, consider doing so now while you are able.

- Do you know a CFP® professional? Is this a person you trust? Do you know how to contact them?
- Do you have an Attorney? Is this a person you trust? When was the last time you spoke to or contacted your attorney? How can they be contacted?
- Do you have a will? Is it up to date?
- Do you have a CPA? Is this a person you trust? When was the last time you spoke to or contacted your CPA? How can they be contacted?
- Do you own a business? Do you have a succession plan? What part in managing your business will you have in retirement? What debts and assets does the business have?
- List family members including spouse, children & grandchildren and any other dependants (i.e. disabled sibling or parent).

- List children and Grandchildren from a former marriage, step-children, or any other descendants not listed above.
- List any people whom you consider immediate family but do not fit into either question above (i.e. live-in friends, favorite cousin, etc.). Think about this is terms of who may take care of you should you fall ill, or for whom you may need to care for in an emergency.
- Do you have a Funeral Plan? Have you purchased a plot? What would you like said at your service? Would you like to be cremated or buried in a traditional casket? Is there anything out of the ordinary that you would like at your funeral? (I once went to a funeral where the deceased had been a Corvette collector and all the drivers from his Corvette Club lined up the cars at the cemetery...)
- Do you have a living will and a healthcare proxy? Who will make decisions for you when/if you no longer can?
- Do you have a Financial Power of Attorney? Who is this person? How can they be contacted?
- Do you have a Healthcare Power of Attorney? Who is this person? How can they be contacted?
- How large is your estate? Do you have other properties besides your main residence? Do you own commercial investment property? Where are these properties located?
- Do you have any prenuptial or postnuptial agreements? Do you have any other long term financial commitments to people/institutions?
- Do you have a gifting plan? Is there a charity that should benefit from your generosity? Would you like to set up a trust or other entities?
- Do you have Health Care Insurance or a health care supplement? You need to know all of the facts and make sure you have the documentation organized.
- Do you have Long Term Care Insurance? What kind of coverage do you have? Is this enough to cover you if you need to go into a long-term hospice or hospital stay?
- Do you have Life Insurance? How much? What kind of Life Insurance does your spouse have? Who is the policy holder?
- List any debts: credit cards, mortgages, car loans, etc.

- List your Property and Causality Insurance along with Umbrella Insurance. Who are the carriers? When was the last time you had your policies reviewed?
- List your checking and saving accounts: Which banks do you currently have accounts in, and what are the balances?
- Have you chosen a place in which to retire? Have you thought about what you want? Do you have a specific location, i.e. a home, or a State, i.e. Arizona? Would you prefer something like a community with amenities or a large property far away from others?
- Are you prepared and physically able to care for your spouse in case of health issues? What preparations can you put in place to make your retirement home easier or better to live in during your later years, i.e. larger doorways, handicap accessible showers, etc?

CHAPTER 5

When it Comes to Retirement...
Everything Matters

Have you ever considered retiring early? Are there benefits to waiting? There are many variables that can affect retirement before age sixty-five, everything from health care to federal guidelines. The decision is yours. However, the decision of being able to retire balances on knowing what your options and consequences will be.

This chapter will discuss the following areas:

- Investment Location
- Social Security Benefits
- When Should You Retire?
- What is a "Normal" Retirement?
- What Do You Really Need?
- Prepare for the Future
- Save Now...Save Later
- Never Outlive Your Savings
- Retirement 101
- Pensions Are Dead
- Tax Efficiency
- Get Help... There's Nothing Wrong with That!

Investment Location

First, locate the best place for your investments—and by that, I really mean "places." New tax laws have reduced the taxes you pay on certain types of investments. It may be beneficial to save through both tax-deferred and taxable accounts. Your advisor should have options available for you, to give you the best opportunities for financial growth. My philosophy, which I discussed earlier, is "get your boats in the water." I advocate a strategic and custom plan of multiple types of investments; so that you are carried through the rough waters to your destination! (And if you are fortunate, your money lives on long after you, to help support your surviving family members.) How many boats should you have: four, six, or ten? Should a speedboat be a part of your portfolio? What is your risk level and what is your investment return requirement? These are great questions to ask your representative.

Investments such as bonds that provide regular income may be a better place to hold stock investments that pay capital gains and dividends. Even though you pay taxes every year, the tax rate may be lower. There are many different types of these investments available today; some are much more aggressive than others. Tax laws are a "moving target" and they change often. A great investment today could be the worst investment tomorrow based on taxation and risk variables. These investments are not suitable for everyone. It is important to work with a Financial Professional that will help to guide you through your goals and objectives.

Guard against inflation:

Remain Diversified: "Keep Your Boats in the Water"	Review Your Portfolio Regularly & Rebalance as necessary	Understand Retirement Planning is a Long-Term Commitment

Social Security Benefits

Americans think of Social Security as their safety net—you would be better off to think of it as a nice bonus if you've planned correctly. Social Security doesn't guarantee you will have enough money to live comfortably, but it is counted on by many Americans today. In fact, Social Security should just be one small component of a healthy retirement plan. Furthermore, this government-run system is in its own financial trouble. It is likely that generations to come won't get their full benefit because of age adjustments and the fact that people are living longer.

Currently, you may start receiving Social Security Benefits at age 62, no matter what your full-retirement age. However, your benefits will be permanently reduced by 20-30% depending on your normal retirement age and how early you retire. If you compare this to the option of working until age 70, your total reduction is more than double. It is important to know what your Social Security benefits really are, and how what you do can affect them. Remember this should be just one part of your long-term strategy. If you try to rely entirely on Social Security, you will be disappointed (and probably broke!). Please sit down with your CFP® professional and set up a game plan for withdrawing initial Social Security benefits. If you are married and your wife's parents lived a long life, you may want to take benefits later so that your spouse will receive the maximum at your death. There are a multiple of options to choose from.

To calculate your future Social Security benefits using an online benefit calculator, go to: http://www.socialsecurity.gov/planners

Year of Birth	Full Retirement Age
1937 (or earlier)	65
1938	65 and 2 months
1939	65 and 4 months
1940	65 and 6 months
1941	65 and 8 months
1942	65 and 10 months
1943-1954	66
1955	66 and 2 months
1956	66 and 4 months
1957	66 and 6 months
1958	66 and 8 months
1959	66 and 10 months
1960 (or later)	67

Refer to the previous year if you were born on January 1.
Source: Social Security Administration Online.

Social Security is a substantial benefit. If you look at attempting to maintain a $24,000 per annum payout for life, a lump sum of $480,000 is needed based on a 5% payout ratio. A sum of $600,000 is needed based on a 4% payout ratio. This shows the importance of Social Security for most Americans who may not have saved this example of $600,000 for their retirement.

For the skeptics that assume they should take Social Security early because of family history, I understand. You may want to look closer into the health issues that your family has had in the past to find out if controlling present high blood pressure and cholesterol would possibly change your life expectancy. Talk to your Doctor and get their opinion to better judge this question. I hope this section has showed the importance of saving, money management, and choosing your Financial Professional. I wonder why our government wants to control healthcare...I'll let you read between the lines!

When Should Your Retire?

No one wants to work forever. When you actually can (or should) retire depends on a number of factors: your anticipated future lifestyle, what you would like to do in retirement, and how much money you have saved. Before you choose your retirement age, you will need to think about your needs, wants, current situation, and where your life and money may be down the road.

There are often definite advantages to delaying retirement. Some companies and professions still offer pensions that become active after you reach a particular age. If you are able to stick with it (if this is your case), then you should. Social Security will become available to you at 62; but to receive full retirement benefits and avoid penalties, you will have to wait. The same may be true for your job—so educate yourself and do some careful consideration about when is a good time! It is better to wait a year or two now, while you have the option, than find yourself looking for a new job in 10 years ... and unfortunately that happens all too often.

This again is a double edged sword. Those that can retire in their fifties seem to live a healthier lifestyle if they have prepared monetarily. I believe that the stress of having to work in our sixties can take years off of our lifespan. Both emotionally and physically, stress does kill.

What is a "Normal" Retirement?

Your retirement may be spent at a festive beach home in Mexico, or an upscale condo in New York City, or a quaint and quiet farm in Idaho. You may want to travel to exotic places like Morocco, Rome, Egypt, and Paris ... or you may just want to enjoy a half acre of land with a pond. The concept of **"normal"** varies from person to person, but the best normal retirement is one where the individual or couple never <u>has</u> to take the option of going back to work once they do decide to retire. Working part time at an art gallery or as a nursery school teacher may be the dream retirement that you choose; however, it's your choice. Working because you enjoy it is much different than having to work to live.

To have what is considered a normal retirement, you should be financially stable to support yourself and your spouse in the way that you have lived your lives to that point. Normal should include being happy with being retired, having the time to do the things you have wished you could do, the way you would like to do them. Retirement should be a time when you have the freedom to make the decisions you want to make ... you have earned it!

What Do You Really Need?

What will you need to enjoy your retirement years to their fullest? You certainly should meet your needs—but also a good portion of your wants. However, there is a difference! It may help to make a list of your monthly and annual expenses to get a clear idea of how much you'll need to live day to day. Budgeting is a difficult task, but needed.

Needs	Wants
• Food	• Consumer Items
• Housing & Utilities	• Travel and Entertainment
• Medical	• Gifts
• Taxes	• Charitable Donations
• Insurance	

Once you have the better idea of how much you will need; you can think about how long you'll need to continue saving to reach your goal and ultimately determine your retirement age. Later there is a worksheet where you can comprehensively list what your current expenses are and separate your needs vs. wants.

Prepare for the Future

If you plan to work part-time in your retirement, pursue a second career, or use your new-found time to do volunteer work—you are a part of a growing trend! Seventy percent of workers over the age of 50 plan to remain very active after retirement[1]. The desire to remain active, along with medical advancements and healthier lifestyles has contributed to increased life expectancy. The bottom line: you could spend more than 20 years in retirement. What will these 20 years look like and how can you prepare? The choices you make now can have a dramatic effect on how you will spend two decades—or more! **How are your boats positioned?**

The other day a friend of mine was out for a walk in her neighborhood. There was an older gentleman in a driveway trying to get his wife out of the car and into a wheelchair. The wife, who was diabetic and had a recent stroke, had to have surgery to remove her toes. She spent two months in rehab, the maximum allowed by Medicare for her situation. The husband had gotten her home and was clearly struggling to maneuver her to the chair, so my friend ran over to help.

As my friend helped, she learned this couple's story. Lucille had been diabetic for years, and had not managed her disease. She had gained considerable weight and had undoubtedly long-since given up on taking care of herself. The man had no one to help him bathe his wife, or get her to the bed. He did not know how long he had with his wife, and bringing her home was bittersweet. As my friend told me this sad story, I thought about what could have been done to avoid a woman in her 70's having to go through the pain of surgery and the subsequent indignity and frustration of having to have her husband take care of her basic—and medical needs. The last weeks or months of this woman's life would likely be spent miserably. Her husband would try his best, and unfortunately this would not be enough.

Now, I don't know the whole story; and certainly it is hard to speculate about all the things that led up to this. I do know that I never want to be in Lucille's shoes. I am going to stay healthy and active, work extra hard at maintaining a good diet—take the medications that I need. Most of all, I am going to make sure my wife will have help caring for me should life twist that way.

Investing for a happy and healthy retirement is a lovely thing, but investing for an unhealthy one is important too. You may need additional care, help with basic needs or special medical attention. Preparing now, by staying well as long as possible, and finding a good independent advisor associate to help you invest in a future is profoundly important! You do not need to be in a situation where you are sent home after surgery before you can care for yourself, with the only help available an elderly spouse to look after you the way Lucille did.

"Staying Ahead of the Curve 2004: The AARP Working in Retirement Study" American Association of Retired Persons, October 2004.

Save Now...Save Later

If there is only one thing that you take away from this book, it is this: contribute to your employer-sponsored retirement plan now! If you can, contribute the maximum amount allowed—the IRS limit is $18,000. In addition, if you are age 50 or older, you may be able to make a catch-up contribution of $6,000. These guidelines are a moving target going forward. Try to maximize as much as you are able. Never forget the silent killer ... **Inflation!**

Then continue to contribute to an IRA later! Today you can save up to $5,500 with a $1,000 catch-up limit into a Traditional IRA. When you retire from your full-time job, you may continue working; but you may not be eligible to participate in the company's retirement plan. If you are eligible, look into rolling over your account balance in an employer-sponsored retirement plan into an IRA and make regular contributions. You'll continue to benefit from tax-deferred compounding.

I am going to repeat myself one more time ... Get help and find a CFP® professional today. There are a multiple of different types of Qualified Plans. Each has different rules when it comes to contributions and qualifications. You do not want to make a mistake when it comes to this kind of planning. This, like many tax laws, is a moving target. Rules change often and your Financial Professional will keep up with these changes.

The majority of people don't save the way they should. Making contributions that occur automatically to a retirement plan will help you to save without thinking about it. Each month you should be putting something away; it should be the maximum amount that you can afford. No one is ever disappointed when they have "extra" money; but plenty of people are devastated when they haven't saved enough to retire.

For the young readers: if you're structured enough ... save early and often. Contribute to your 401K especially if there is a match (free money). If you don't have a 401K, start an IRA for you and your spouse. Pensions are just about dead so you will need to max out everything possible. Unfortunately, Social Security will definitely become an issue for the young. It will be revamped and probably readjusted so that you will have to work longer and possibly receive a smaller benefit.

Along with this forced savings for retirement. The young will need an emergency fund that can handle six to nine months of bills. Usually when that refrigerator goes out, two or three other things break at the same time … I don't know why this happens. Loss of a job by either spouse is unfortunately always a possibility.

Also, start some type of a non qualified tax deferral plan that may help with retirement or other issues later in life. This will allow you to tactically manage non IRA monies avoiding yearly taxation until the cash is needed. Most Americans won't be able to maintain their lifestyle by only saving just the norm! By the way … **don't forget about college for your kids!**

Find a CFP® professional early in life that you like and trust. Someone that is close to your age and will be around a long time. One of my clients last week had to have a "heart to heart" with his doctor. He just realized that when he gets close to needing Medicare, his doctor will have already retired. **Right when he needs him the most.** Today, he is looking for a new doctor that's younger and plans on being around for a long time.

Never Outlive Your Savings

I hear this a lot today … People fear waking up during their later years broke and still vital and healthy—having to face the possibility of trying to find work and support themselves for another 10, 15, 20 or more years.

Can you imagine having a decent account balance at age 65 only to wake up ten years later broke? That is a kind of pain that I hope none of my clients ever experience! When I think about the injustices of aging without adequate financial resources; I always picture my beloved grandmother's kitchen with that old time metal table and chairs. Too many days were spent sitting at the table talking to me about how she would love to make ice cream or homemade bread but couldn't afford it. It was heartbreaking.

My Grandmother being unable to do something nice for a grandchild is a depressing situation; however, outliving your savings is dramatically worse. As I have already discussed: life expectancies have grown and retirements have lengthened. In 1950, people expected to be retired for up to 8 years. Today, many people are retired for 20 years, or more! **PLAN**

Retirement 101

Do you want to retire early at 55 or 60? It sounds like a great idea, right? Nevertheless, this is before the safety net of Social Security or Medicare benefits would normally kick in; so should you? Early retirement is a dream for many, and with some careful planning and investing; this dream can come true. But you need the crash course: "Retirement 101."

You will very likely read that you need 60% of your pre-retirement income to enjoy a comfortable retirement at a similar standard to that which you have been living in pre-retirement. However, since the earliest retirement income comes from taxable sources, 80% is very likely a more realistic figure.

Now, if you want to live in a more "active" lifestyle, travel or have a second home, you should plan on 90% or more. If you retire early, most of you will have to provide for all of your health and income needs from your own resources. Some options include:

- Company or government defined benefit pension plan (if they provide early retirement benefits and aren't in financial straits, as many currently are).
- Defined contribution lump sums, 401(k)s, and other qualified retirement plan funds such as IRAs and 403(b)s.
- Personal investments (including non-retirement annuities, mutual funds, stocks, bonds, CDs and cash).
- Proceeds from the sale of a home, or investment property.
- Part-time work and spouse's income.

Retirement 101

- Plan on living longer than the charts show… so you have to be optimistic and conservative, and your money needs to last.
- Plan on medical insurance premiums and medical costs rising much faster than inflation. Look at additional options such as long-term care insurance.
- Plan on long-term care costs and insurance rising much, much faster than inflation, so invest early, and save often!
- Plan on guaranteeing lifetime income for at least a portion of your needs – you don't want to outlive your retirement "nest egg." The extra cost will have significant ROI.
- Don't be under-budget. Retirement is not cheap – especially if you want a second home and an active lifestyle, and/or wish to travel.
- Do not "dip" into your retirement to solve a short-term debt problem. This will cost more than it could ever save.
- Be careful in choosing entirely fixed income. Investment options such as bonds, traditional annuities and CDs will not likely give your principle a chance to grow and keep pace with inflation. These are good for diversification, but not as a plan themselves.
- Be careful when choosing only "plain vanilla" investing. A large stock market can devastate a retirement portfolio, so have your game plan in place and get your "boats in the water."
- Don't count on inheritances, you never know when Aunt Millie may die and if she really did think of you as her favorite.
- Continue to invest for growth, not purely for income. Think big.
- Don't count on being in a lower tax bracket. Tax law changes, your income may be greater than you expected— there are too many factors to play this game, so always assume you will be paying more.

Pensions Are Dead

Years ago, you as a faithful employee would work for a company for twenty to thirty years and in return for your hard work and loyalty, would get a nice fat pension to live out your retirement. This Pension was a defined-benefit plan guaranteed by your employer to usually pay a monthly check until death. At that time, if you selected the correct option, your spouse would then receive a check for their lifetime. This type of plan put the entire risk of market performance on the company. It also meant that the company itself had to maintain strength in their industry and stay solvent. If the company went under ... your pension went under. **A PENSION IS A PROMISE!**

Earlier in chapter 3, we had discussed annuities and how they could guarantee a check for life. In some situations, the insurance company is holding the risk for market performance along with you. If your account was to go to zero prior to your death, the insurance company would continue to send you and your spouse a check for life (there again if you chose the spousal option). In some cases, you can maintain an allocation in the markets and also hold a lifetime payment until death. Insurance companies usually maintain reserves for their living guarantees.

OK, so if you are fortunate enough to have a pension, you still have to look out for the fact that it will lose "value" over time. It's usually a fixed monthly check without an increase for inflation. It's taxable, and probably not large enough to supply the required income that you and your spouse may need.

But hey ... if you have a pension, you are one of the lucky ones!

This is a fact: your children and grandchildren will likely never have the opportunity to have a pension. And those who may have been promised one in the last decade or so, cannot really count on it even existing today, let alone in thirty years. Even if you're a Government worker...is your pension secure? Many pension funds have gone bankrupt. Effectively, pensions are a thing of the past; a way for businesses to reward their employees and keep them around their entire working lives. Yet, businesses are not run that way anymore. Companies don't seem to care about long-term relationships with their employees...again - this concept of relationships has evaporated. Pensions are dead--along with customer service, chivalry, and the fifty cent malt shake. Count yourself lucky if you find any of these!

Tax Efficiency

Structuring the retirement income stream to minimize taxation in retirement is an important objective. By choosing the various sources of funds carefully – mixing funds that are tax deferred, tax free, taxed at capital gains rates, and taxed at income tax rates – it is possible to increase net income from a pool of money. This may help to avoid a significant loss due to taxation.

You may choose to defer the taxes on an investment until retirement. A tax-deferred investment is one for which you pay federal and state income taxes when withdrawals are made during retirement, rather than during the accumulation phase when the money is invested and managed accordingly. Any earnings your contributions produce while they remain invested are also tax deferred.

Some investments allow you to invest pre-tax dollars; so neither the contribution nor its potential earnings are taxed until they are withdrawn. Let's look at an example to show the importance of avoiding yearly taxation in an account that may be tactically managed. An investment of $200,000 growing deferred for 20 years with an 8% rate of return, would grow to approximately $930,000. That same investment in a 39.6% tax bracket each year may equate to as low as approximately $510,000. This shows the importance of tax deferral, which leaves a substantially larger amount to withdraw from during retirement, almost doubling your income.

This debate is discussed often among the many Financial Professionals, especially the ones that dislike annuities. (Usually these are the guys that work in the large brokerage houses and prejudge what they've never learned … we don't know what we don't know.) I feel that it's impossible to effectively manage a taxable brokerage account knowing that clients may be taxed on every move.

Many individuals state that currently capital gains taxes are lower than regular income taxes … I would have to reply to find out what portion of the portfolio will be held for at least one year to receive these benefits. At that point, don't you want to have the availability to sell a position early and avoid loss? I would! I think that it's also hard to tactically sell winners and losers and negate profits and lower taxation … we are trying to make a profit, aren't we? Capital gains taxes are a "moving target" subject to increase at the drop of a dime. If we look at investing as long term, why look at taxation short term? **Just one man's opinion.**

Get Help ... There's Nothing Wrong with That!

If you haven't guessed by now ... I think we all need a Financial Professional in our lives. I have the honor of being that person for my clients; however, I find it sad that some folks are not comfortable with sharing their financial situations, or personal stories, with others.

In my opinion, there is nothing wrong with getting help when it comes to investing for your retirement. Find someone you trust, like, and enjoy talking to. Some people are embarrassed to ask for help, or are untrusting. I understand! That is why you need to work with someone that cares about you and your family and isn't afraid to be 100% honest with your goals and fears.

Pro athletes have coaches. Even the best, most accomplished business people have advisors. The president has a cabinet—even Oprah has Gayle! Tiger Woods, Phil Michelson, and even the legendary Jack Nicklaus had coaches. You don't have to go it alone when it comes to planning and investing for your retirement.

The key is to find the person that best understands you and your needs. That can sometimes be difficult; but I challenge you to make that happen for you and your family. It is always okay to ask for help when you need it. You can't possibly know everything. That's a lot of responsibility!

CHAPTER 6

The Ten Deadly Sins of Investing

Investment mistakes are made daily - everything from procrastinating to being blinded by what is right in front of you ("inside the snow globe"). If you're too close to a situation, you're blinded. Why do you think surgeons are not allowed to operate on family, too much emotion blinds both good judgment and good thinking at the same time. These are the 10 Deadly Sins of Investing.

This chapter will discuss the following areas:

- Procrastination
- The Problems with Vanilla
- Going Solo
- Chasing Returns
- Not Knowing When to Let Go
- Fear of Change
- Monday Morning Quarterbacks Always Win
- Staying Behind the Ball
- Lack of Inflation Knowledge
- Inside the Snow Globe

Procrastination

Stocks and bonds are up, and then they are down. It is scary ... so you decide to wait. And wait. Of all the "sins" of investing, this one is the most pervasive and "deadly." Time and compounding are always the largest compliments of investments; and to delay, even just an annual deduction of $12,000 to a 401(k) for only 5 years, can mean a huge reduction in the money you could have available at retirement. At a conservative assumed rate of return of 8% for 20 years instead of 25 years you could potentially have lost hundreds of thousands of dollars.

| $12,000/year | 8% | 20 Years | Ending value: ~ $590,000 |
| $12,000/year | 8% | 25 Years | Ending value: ~ $950,000 |

In this scenario the cost of delaying by just a few years is $360,000 for the additional $60,000 investment, a net loss of $300,000 with compounding. Today you can contribute a maximum of $18,000 per year with a $6,000 catch up for those over 50 into your 401K. Contribute as much you can afford, especially if there is a company match.

Many families make the mistake of spending more time planning that one family vacation than planning their entire retirement future—and the result could be drastic for your nest egg. It may take you as little as one hour for you to find the right CFP® professional that will guide you on your way. **Small changes could make huge results for your future!**

The Problems with Vanilla

Ok, by now you think that you know what **"Plain Vanilla Investing"** is and you're probably tired of reading about it. However, do you really understand the *problems* with vanilla? Essentially, if your representative can only offer you a small selection of products, they are doing you a disservice. They are withholding options from you - options that could make or break your future. Options that could help you to survive a devastating market crash or another **"Great Depression."**

To establish a major fleet of boats... you must have an entire list of different options available. You aren't like everyone else—and you may not even have the same needs you did five years ago, or possibly will in five years. The problem with vanilla is that it is always just that... **just vanilla.** Sometimes it will work; but most of the time, you want—you need—something a little more custom. You might need chocolate swirl with caramel chunks, chocolate chips, and whipped cream in a waffle cone! A submarine may be required if a hurricane is in the forecast ... What will you do if the only option is a slow sailboat? Will a hurricane destroy your future? Why would you invest in this fashion?

I think this is the toughest conversation that I can have with an individual. They have seen thousands of television advertisements and heard hundreds of hours of radio produced by proprietary companies. When a CFP® professional discusses with a new client the differences between proprietary vs. independent Financial Professionals, it's tough to comprehend. Hopefully this chapter will help!

Going Solo

A few people honestly believe that they can save money and get better performance by handling their investments themselves. And in truth, maybe they can. (That is, if they really want to work that hard during their second half of life.) However, unless you are extremely disciplined and spend many hours educating yourself; preparing and following asset allocation and investment strategies, researching and making investing your primary occupation, and are able to make decisions without letting emotion sway you—it is easy to fall victim to one or more of the **Ten Daily Sins.**

By the way…some of the boats needed to survive a twenty to thirty year retirement are not available to purchase without a Financial Professional. You will need help to look into the many variables and make the correct choices.

While there are no guarantees when it comes to investment performance; the knowledge and years of experience from a trained and dedicated Financial Professional is extremely valuable. The resources, assistance, and benefits such as strategic management, tactical management, asset allocation, and other features may help minimize various forms of investment-related risk and be invaluable. **ONCE AGAIN** … by going solo, the average investor will never see the advisor programs that are solely available through Investment Advisor Representative conduits. Many of the Submarine, Speedboat, and Aircraft Carriers are attainable through advisor channels only.

Going solo can be dangerous, and could have a serious negative effect on your ability to maintain yourself through your retirement.

Chasing Returns
Driving While Looking in the Rear View Mirror

One of the biggest temptations of the solo investor is the tendency to "chase returns"—buy the stock or fund that returned 15% last quarter or 30% the last three years. If you look through the various consumer financial and money magazines from one, five, or ten years ago, you will quickly discover it's the rare fund or stock that makes the Top Ten list two or more years in a row. Buying what is hot today is too often a ticket to a loss tomorrow. Past performance is not a guarantee of future results. **Buying high and selling low is dangerous!**

Exceptional returns over one period are frequently followed by losses in the next. In the years 1999 and 2000, there was a sharp rise and fall of the NASDAQ. In 1999 the NASDAQ Composite Index returned an extraordinary 86%. If you had "chased" this return by investing in the index at the beginning of 2000, you would have been in for a sharp disappointment. In 2000, the NASDAQ Composite Index returned - 39%, and in 2001 and 2002 it returned -21% and -31% respectively. A $10,000 investment in the NASDAQ Index at the end of 1999 would have been worth only $3,307 at the end of 2002. Even if you had invested at the beginning of 1999, experiencing the 86% gain, your $10,000 investment would have been worth $6,136 at the end of 2002.

There is an important point to remember. Short-term extraordinary gains are not reliable. It is unfair to judge your representative by looking at highs in the market and expecting this euphoria to remain consistent. However, by sticking to a carefully thought out investment strategy, you increase your chance of taking advantage of the historical returns that come with investing in equities. Just remember that long-term returns for the market as a whole have been positive. So avoid overreacting to short-term changes and focus on the long term picture.

Rather than succumbing to greed and chasing only top performers, it is advisable to take an asset managed approach to keep portfolios in balance with risk tolerance and long-term investment goals. This is my model for a modern day sailboat using high tech weather equipment. Let's take it one step further and make planned, regular investments to even out the ups and downs of the market. This can be a great way to handle rough seas and hurricanes. I used it often for the market volatility earlier last decade.

Not Knowing When to Let Go

Emotionally, it's very difficult for individuals to not only admit they made a mistake; but also put it in writing. Having to sell a stock at a loss is the same as putting it in writing. Buying and selling stocks in general is a tough proposition for many...and way too emotional for most. Having to sell a loser is impossible for some and painful for others. I knew many happy "day traders" in the 1990's when the market was good and the volatility was low. It was easy for most...even a chimpanzee. Their happiness was unfortunately short lived when the volatility of the past decade increased. **Many lost their shirts.**

Numerous wealthy business owners will use margin to day-trade. This is very risky and many lost extensive cash when the market turned in 2000. When I discuss day-trading with many investors today; most admit that by the year end, they usually lose money.

I can tell you one story about a young man that sold his business and cleared over two million dollars in the mid-nineties. The next day he bought a high dollar tech stock worth 60 dollars a share. He purchased 10,000 shares. Yes, for the math majors, this is $600,000 worth of just one stock ... **scary!** The next day the stock began to fall 5 dollars, then 8 dollars, then 15 dollars. He didn't know what to do...he was down $150,000 in just one day and decided to <u>hold on</u>. The end of this story isn't good. Nine months later he sold his stock at a 10 dollar value showing a loss of $500,000. He was devastated. He didn't want to admit he'd made a mistake and held on too long. This emotion makes investment losses hard to face.

The investment ideology of buying one company stock and holding it for many years may be absurd today. *(At least with your serious money.)* Look at Enron, for example. To add to this, some may feel that by owning many different types of company stocks, they may lower their loss in case of a problem. Unfortunately, the world of today seems to be moving in sync, making this a tougher task. Owning one stock is comparable to riding in an elevator to the one hundredth floor of a high rise using only one thin cable **(a little scary).** Wouldn't you rather have one hundred or even one thousand cables? I would! Maybe you'll get lucky with this one cable for one or two years. But long term, it is risky and how much risk do you take with your family's future? *Letting go is hard to do when we make a mistake.*

Fear of Change

Going it alone can frequently mean "not investing at all" or being too conservative in predicting your future income needs and goals. It can lead to keeping hundreds of thousands of dollars in short-term investments, savings accounts, and money market accounts during your prime earnings and accumulation years.

I recently talked to a gentleman that had been in treasuries for the entire year of 2009 while the market dramatically increased. He only received a return of 2% while many investors were receiving returns in excess of 20% in conservative portfolios. Can you imagine how much an 18% larger return could have helped his portfolio and financial position? Fear of getting back in the market can be devastating. Investors seem to find it difficult to understand the negative effects that inflation can do to a portfolio. This is the reason why I designed the "multiple boats philosophy." Many of my clients have over eight different types of vessels in the waters at all times. A submarine and aircraft carrier can do wonders in poor investment conditions.

For many, the **"fear of change,"** when it comes to investments or Financial Professionals, can become an issue. It is concerning how many individuals try to justify staying with their current representative when their account balance is the same today as it was in 1999. Seven years of flat performance equals a loss of 31% based on a 4% inflation rate. Fear of change causes some investors to hesitate and miss opportunities—opportunities to grow their wealth and succeed.

Monday Morning Quarterbacks Always Win

What is the old saying "Hindsight is 20/20?" Looking back on a past decision, it is a lot easier to see what the right answer should have been. Being in "the moment" emotion can sometimes cloud your ability to be objective. The "emotion of the moment" is not the correct way to manage your money—yet so many do-it-yourselfers fall into this trap of seeing how things have happened in the past, and then find themselves looking back wishing they had done things differently.

The emotion of managing your own money, watching the daily swings of the stock market, and seeing others struggle, can make even the most confident and emotionally stable person double check themselves constantly. Looking back and trying to redefine a market that is "manic at times" is truly impossible.

By allowing yourself the benefit of a Financial Professional, you can put a barrier in between you and quick emotional reactions. Your advisor should be able to balance the need to make a change if one is warranted with a thoughtful and strategic process. Having many boats in the water will decrease your "gut shot" reaction to make changes. This will better your chances to have the retirement that you dream of.

Staying Behind the Ball

Imagine you are out for your daily walk in the snow during the holidays. The day is cold, gray, and damp. You look up and see a massive snow ball, ten feet in diameter, quickly rolling down the hill. This gigantic ball of ice is heavy and very dangerous—and it is coming into the populated valley below.

Now, think of the ball as the stock market. It is moving at maximum volatility with tremendous market swings occurring daily; sometimes, for no reason at all. Is the volatility caused by big banks, congress making changes to trading rules, congress making changes to accounting rules, or radical traders? Is the volatility being caused by derivatives, leverage, or option plays? The investment world will follow behind this ball closely as it rolls down this hill. However, the investment world will never get in front of it ... **no matter what**. No one will risk stepping in front and stopping this massive problem as it is gaining speed. This is why governments always tend to "kick the can down the road"... Gee-whiz, don't you wonder?

Looking at the investment world of today, do you know who's truly in charge? <u>No</u>. To be honest, I really don't know either! However, what I do know is that whoever they are, they would rather pick up the pieces instead of stop a catastrophe. We've all seen this. Do you really think the bubble in 2000 was unforeseen? Don't you believe that the real-estate and mortgage bubble fiasco were predicted? Wake up!

Now, I'm not a full conspiracy nut. But, I did enjoy the television series "X Files." The reason revolves around the fact that no one (governments, companies, individuals, or the financial world) wants to take the risk of changing direction mid-stream and potentially being wrong. Heck, you can see this today when it comes to terrorists and our responses to their violence. I hope one day these threats will be eliminated for good, but I doubt it. We're not the country we were one hundred years ago when we fought for justice and the **"American Way."**

Many changes that were put into place during the first decade of the twenty-first century caused the problems. Too much government and we lose rights and freedoms. Our capital system, if left alone, will tend to solve problems on its own. A poor product will stop being bought, while bad publicity can put an end to a company. Capitalism is the concept that made us this great nation...I hope we can hold on.

Some good examples of government causing problems are the changing of the "uptick rule" and the "mark to market" valuations. Both caused severe market disturbances that were in fact, forecasted. So, who is driving the bus? I assume ... Big Business, Big Money, and Big Lobbyists ... along with the power that government officials are addicted to. Just one man's opinion!

Clearly, no one wants to take the blame for plummeting market conditions. No one wants to take the blame for losing their client's retirements. Nevertheless, there are ways and opportunities to stop all of this drama! Yet, they aren't taken. I don't know; but I do think that it is soberly unfortunate.

Take the example of the market collapse of 2000-2002. I watched the market fall daily and was being told by my bosses to hold the course. We were instructed to keep our clients invested. At that time, the powers that be were afraid to make a judgment and discuss cash or inverse positioning. I understand their thought process – a mass exodus out of the market would prove to be devastating. But for most older investors, it could have been a financial life saver. Buy and hold strategies tend to work long term; but for our retirees or soon-to-be retirees ... the game changes.

Another analogy: putting the fox in command of the hen house. Why would any company tell their advisors to pull money from the firm and decrease profits for the firm? If one was to put the client first, I believe that many advisors would actually look at secondary investments. Alternative boats designed to react to market volatility and possibly make a profit in poor conditions. The problem with this however, is that many proprietary firms may not give their Financial Professionals this option. Their client maintains an investment doomed to fail ... especially short term. What do your current submarines or aircraft carriers look like?

Lack of Inflation Knowledge

I visit with many soon-to-be retirees and discuss the inflation factor. Too often, they tend to look at me with an "awkward expression." The income amount that they wish to receive at retirement is almost double the current dollar amount of today. As I walked them through our **"world of inflation"** showing their income need increasing yearly, it surprises them. It is very easy to forget this fact. Inflation is the **"silent killer."** I just sat with a family last week. He and his wife had decided on an income amount that they will need later in life, but they used today's dollars. When I told them what their future income need should be … you could have heard a pin drop.

In my younger days, I would show investors the ten cent stamp from the seventies and compare it the stamps in the nineties. Looking at inflation, we can see that a standard-rate First Class 10 cent stamp from the seventies had tripled to a 33 cent stamp by the nineties. In the blink of an eye this 33 cent stamp has gone to 49 cents, and they say that we have little inflation today. Who's kidding who? Check out some cost of living statistics from 1980:

Cost of Living: United States 1980	
Average Cost of a New House	$68,700
Average Income Per Year	$19,500
Average Monthly Rent	$300
Gallon of Gas	$1.19
Average Price of a New Car	$7,200
First Class Stamp	$0.15
Dozen Eggs	$0.91
Gallon of Milk	$2.16

Inside the Snow Globe

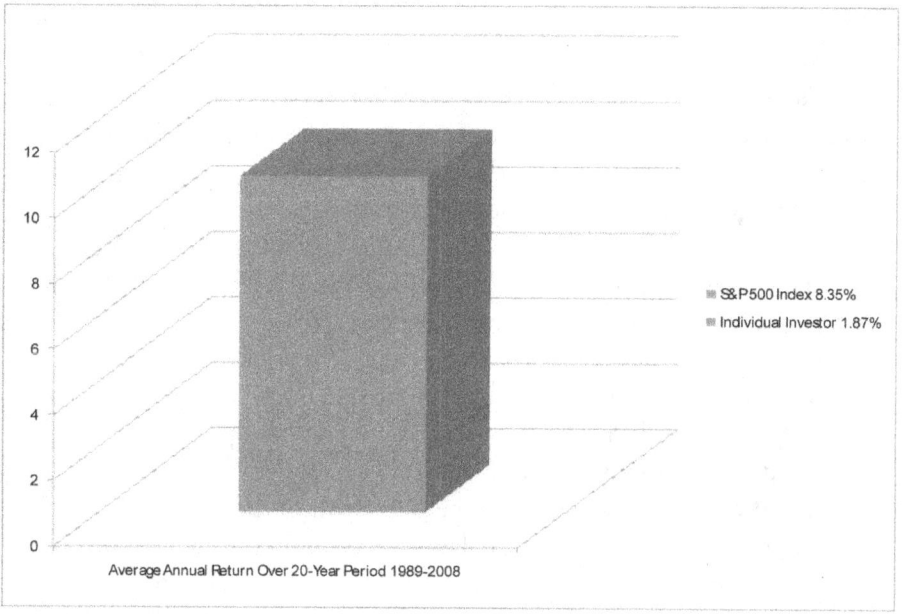

Average Annual Return Over 20-Year Period 1989-2008

■ S&P500 Index 8.35%
■ Individual Investor 1.87%

Remember how your mind worked when you were young - I guess between the ages of three and twelve when everything is shiny, new, exciting, and filled with curiosity? I do (well barely!). At that age, you see things through the eyes of a naive youth with little concept of the big picture. Our lack of knowledge and experience is so very obvious to most.

As we get a little older, and dare I say "teenager," our family or friends may have seen us in an awkward situation. They try to give us well-meaning advice—tell us to open up our eyes to see what's really going on **(right in front of our face).** Actually, they were trying to help us to see the truth. They didn't want to see us get hurt whether it be physically or emotionally.

As everyone seems to find out at that age, we think that we not only know ... everything, but we also believe that we are ... invincible. We try to fake it as often as possible and act mature and extremely confident. Even as an adult ... it's hard to step away from a situation where we are emotionally involved. It's almost impossible to see ourselves from outside the **picture frame** or from outside my favorite analogy: **"the snow globe."**

Imagine for a moment, looking at one of those large snow globes from the past when you were a very young child—perfect from the inside. I used to love to gently handle these snow globes around Christmas time and then just shake them up! I would let the snow settle and allow my imagination to take me inside. I could almost see and feel the snow falling around me as I walked down the road in this tiny miniature town as if it were my own safe harbor; a wonderful world containing only joy and imagination, a place to go where dreams come true.

Living inside the snow globe is a perfect miniscule place where nothing changes—until someone comes along to shake the globe up again (and then it's just snow falling). Inside the globe, we are closed off to the reality of life. All we can see and understand is what's directly in front of us. We're not only invincible, but we can make this imaginary dream world anything we wish. We have little or no perspective of the total picture. We're too close and our emotions are too high.

The investment world is the same way. Most of the time, without the help from a Financial Professional, large mistakes may happen. While you are in the emotion of the stock market—in that **"snow globe,"** you can feel like things are perfect, even when the people around you are telling you to watch out for a big shake-up coming around the corner. Hindsight is 20/20!

*Source: "Quantitative Analysis of Investor Behavior," Dalbar 2009.

Average equity mutual fund investor as measured by Dalbar, Inc. Dalbar derives the average equity fund investor return using a proprietary model that measures actual historical mutual fund returns and average shareholder holding periods. Past performance is no guarantee of future results. The S&P 500® is a market-value-weighted index of 500 stocks that is generally considered representative of the U.S. large-cap equity market. The index is unmanaged and not available for direct investment.

CHAPTER 7

Self Help May Equal Disaster

The world is filled with a variety of radio and television investment gurus. I call them "marketers" or "talking heads" because their free advice is meant to promote their businesses, not necessarily your financial health. I'm sure as you are reading this, many names are coming to mind. I find it satirical that many of these "talking heads" are multi millionaires trying to give advice to **"the little guy"** who they really don't know or care about.

This chapter will discuss the following areas:

- Self Help May Kill Your Investments
- Marketers vs. Advisors
- The Lawyer and The Defendant
- Kia vs. Lexus
- Value, Value, Value

Self Help May Kill Your Investments

The self-help book industry is a multi-million dollar business. And, it is no wonder; they are usually an entertaining read, and sometimes can give people the knowledge and motivation to do the things they have always wanted—or need to do. Nevertheless, what I usually think of when I consider the self-help genre is that common sitcom plot when the well meaning but bungling husband pulls out a book, reads a couple of pages, and then tries to fix the leaky kitchen sink faucet. You know the story: as the whole house is flooding, he finally calls in a real plumber to fix the mess he just made along with the initial problem.

Readers of Investment self-help books can fall into the same catastrophic scenario when it comes to investing. But with one caveat: waterlogged floors or damaged furniture are fixable, especially with insurance. A thirty percent loss in your portfolio can't be repaired that easily, especially if the money is currently needed. Be careful!

We read a self-help book and try to be what the book says we "can be"—do what it says we "can do." It can be profoundly empowering to read and learn to implement that knowledge successfully. However, you wouldn't want your heart surgeon to do a risky invasive procedure if his only experience was reading a how-to book. No, you would want the doctor who had successfully done the surgery thousands of times. You would want the doctor who had gone to school for eight years and really knew his stuff. In this case "self-help" could literally...**kill you.**

Investing for your retirement is the same way. A self-help book may be a great way to learn how to trim a bonsai tree; or how to drop a few pounds with an innovative exercise and diet regime. Do you really want to use it when it comes to life, death or money? It is best to leave it to the experts—don't "go solo." Leave it to the guys who eat, drink, and consume this stuff daily. Real investment experts sit through investment meetings and talk directly to top management teams weekly. Wouldn't you want <u>someone</u> you can call on a Sunday and ask an investment question of? Wouldn't you want <u>someone</u> that will be honest and give you direction when it comes to your largest investment...**your retirement?**

Marketers vs. Advisors
Believing the Radio and Television Marketers of Today

There are a lot of "talking heads" on radio and television. These people are investment marketers, and self-help promoters. Their jobs are to get ratings, sell commercials, and their own books and videos. Most are not CFP˚ professionals currently working daily to grow the wealth of their clients? And, that is the difference: they are not <u>really</u> looking out for <u>you</u>.

I was driving back home from Chicago about seven years ago, listening to the radio and a well-known radio "investment guru" was talking to an older caller. He quickly asked her the amount of money she had in bonds and what type of bonds she owned. Now he could have then asked her age, risk tolerance, income need, total assets, other investments, main concerns…and a vast variety of other questions that may have given him a greater idea about helping her. Nevertheless, he didn't. Not surprisingly he counseled her to try out his "program." He just gave a fast piece of advice, and then he took the next caller. I wonder what kind of *boats* she had in the water. Did she have a submarine or aircraft carrier? I'll never know because she was certainly not asked and not truly cared for. One additional comment: **Today, he's no longer on the radio!**

The concept that is too often discussed by television and radio personalities is an old theory of using just your age to decide about your bond and fixed income position. You're 60 so you need 60% in bonds. While this may be useful in generalities—it certainly puts all callers in the same bucket…**how absurd is this?**

This is how I see it: what if the client has a family longevity of over 100 years and is 60 years old? Imagine if this client needs to draw a 5% return in normal situations and needs a large average total return to avoid going back to work. How will this client feel if he wakes up at age 75 and sees that his portfolio had not only shrunk, but inflation had killed it? Fixed income investments usually have a tough time keeping up with inflation. Remember this!

The point is this: a Financial Professional with your best interests at heart will sit and talk about your total situation. They will identify your fears, dreams, risk tolerance, and above all, be willing to partner with you on your life journey. They will help you to reach your goals…and hopefully, avoid the pot holes along the way. The "talking head" on the TV or radio does not have the time in 30 seconds in a call-in show to get a comprehensive view of what you need and give you the best customized investment strategy!

The Lawyer and the Defendant

We should all be familiar with the Abraham Lincoln quote: "He who represents himself has a fool for a client."

However, we have seen this happen many times. Someone is arrested for a crime, and then he gets on his high horse and says he will defend himself, which we all know is a mistake. How could a lay-person possibly have the knowledge of an experienced trial attorney? How can someone facing jail time represent themselves in a situation where emotion needs to be steady and controlled? Even a trained lawyer knowing all the laws and legal techniques will find that when the situation is their own, emotion cripples their ability to make good decisions. Unfortunately, people make mistakes like this all the time. They let emotion run the train and usually it wrecks.

Would you represent yourself if your life and freedom were on the line? Do you have the knowledge and ability to make decisions devoid of emotion when it comes to what is best for you?

No, of course you don't. And that is why when it comes to your wealth, your future, your financial well-being, you need someone who can use their significant training and expertise to help you. They have perspective and balance while keeping your fleet on the correct course.

Kia vs. Lexus

I want to start by apologizing to all the Kia car owners... this is just an example of getting what we pay for. I do realize that there are a few exceptions. Kia has a significant market share and is a fine vehicle for many people ...

I personally have a 1999 Lexus. It is a beauty of a car with a whopping 305,000 miles on it. I would drive it on a 1,000 mile road trip and not blink an eye. The Lexus came with a hefty price-tag, and I have driven it faithfully for 14 years. The weight and feel of the car make it seem like it could handle any road course around the world. The quality of the workmanship is awesome and I believe it may go for another 300,000 miles. I hope so, it's primo.

Conversely, the Kia car line has been riddled with recalls, problems and consumer complaints (at least in the early days). You can pick up a new Kia for a song; but I have yet to hear of one running for well over 200,000 miles.

When it comes to the important things in life, we seem to get what we pay for. People are always looking at ways to save some cash now—but what if it ends up costing you in the long run? I had a friend go to the web and complete her corporate charter to save one hundred bucks. Was this a frugal move or a dangerous one? Why not have experts do this and save time and trouble? If the worst case scenario is that you lose your business, home, and life savings - why not pay for the best and get it done correctly?

I find that a lot of prospective customers spend a lot of time looking at what the costs are when it comes to investing. They struggle with percentages and fees; and in all honesty, you can invest for less. You can, but should you? Do you want the Kia of Financial Professionals? Alternatively, do you want the Lexus?

More importantly, if you own an investment vehicle that acts like a Lexus when it comes to dependability and longevity; won't you feel better at age 75 to know it's still going strong.

Seeing the pain on someone's face because they had made a poor decision and purchased an investment only for the low cost, is a sad thing. Waking up at age 75 and envisioning having to go get a job at Wal-Mart as a greeter is even worse. The only conclusion is to talk to a Financial Professional to find out which Lexus type vehicle is best for you. At the end of the day, survival through retirement is your only concern. **Failure isn't an option!**

Value, Value, Value

"Value, value, value." This reminds me of the familiar real estate adage: "location, location, location."

Any investment has an intrinsic value and all investments have a cost. If you were to buy a low cost mutual fund and this fund were purchased prior to a dramatic market fall... Well, you may have just lost a lot of cash, even though your fund fee was minimal. Let's set an example of a low cost yearly fund fee of ½ percent. If the market drops 33% and your fund drops 33.5% with the fee....... are you happy? I don't think so!

If this person had instead hired a CFP® Professional that had a high value, high cost, and saved them from a large market loss - who's happier? If this Advisor Associate helped this investor purchase a submarine, an aircraft carrier, and a multiple of guaranteed investments - Who's happier? If at the end of the day this investor can retire, maintain the income that they desire, and sleep well at night - who's happier? Value may be the most important characteristic of investing, not the cost. Which choice would you make?

Remember the heart surgeon from Chapter 3? What if he tells you that you will get the special "low cost" plan today since he won't be using any experienced doctors for your surgery? How do you feel? Not glad about the "great deal" – that is for sure! When it comes to the important things, it's not about the cost ... it's always about the value.

The "value, value, value" statement really means "you get what you pay for." We never mind paying more for **TRUE VALUE** if it's for the important things in life. If an investor bought a million dollar home in a great location, with the best view, on a beautiful lot; odds are, this is a great value. In contrast: if he had bought a tract home in the middle of nowhere that was valued by the builder's mortgage company; odds are, this is not a great value. If you choose an investment option based on the cost only—it may cost you! Instead, it is consistently better to go with an experienced professional representative with great service and great ideas.

So what makes a good advisor? A good Advisor Associate is one who offers you value. You have to ask: what kind of credentials, experience, and expertise do they have? Are they captive to any particular products, or can they offer you the best choices, regardless of the vendor? Do they believe in the "Multiple Boat Theory"? What kind of licensing do they have? If you want the best, your representative may be more expensive – but that means they may be more qualified. And you must decide if you feel that the value is, or is not, important.

I have learned through the years that, when it comes to investments, you pay more for excellent research and high quality. Is your life worth substantial quality and guarantees or not? Can you imagine your worst fears of waking up at age 75 and looking at a zero balance in your accounts knowing that social security is all you have? That is a huge fear, and certainly not something you want to deal with when it may be too late.

CHAPTER 8

Bigger is Not Always Better

Most individuals combine security and trust in a representative, or advisory company by seeing a large beautiful building in the middle of a city filled with employees. However, does the size of the building, the number of employees, or the large advertising budget have anything to do with how you or your investments will be treated? Do you genuinely believe that seeing this company promoting themselves on television every fifteen minutes during a major sporting event makes them a better choice? Have we gotten to the point where we are totally naïve when it comes to subconscious visual intake? (**Hopefully not.**) I think we've all had issues with "big business" of today and realize, it's truly the opposite … *we're just a number.*

This chapter will discuss the following areas:

- Proprietary vs. Non-Proprietary
- Putting the Client ~~First~~ Last
- The Independent Investment Advisor is the Answer

Proprietary vs. Non-Proprietary

As we have discussed, there are different types of CFP® professionals, Financial Professionals, and Advisor Associates. Finding the right one for you is very important if you want to protect your savings and turn it into an investment.

Most Financial Professionals are agents working for a company that offers a limited selection of plans. These companies usually comprise of either an Insurance Company, Mutual Fund Company, or Bank. These firms are usually solely owned and control the Financial Professional through their back office arrangements. They are married to this company and can only offer a small selection of packages. They are unable to look at the entire universe of investments available for their clients, because of their agreement and because of the compensation that they derive from these options. These are *proprietary* investments.

For example, if you walk into a big bank-backed investment company, you may be offered a variety of just that bank's investment packages. In this sense, the person you are meeting with is less an advisor to you, and more a **salesperson** for that institution. You can't be matched with the perfect, custom, ideal investment strategy, if the person sitting across the desk (or worse – on the phone – or worse – online) has a job of "selling" only a proprietary set of options.

When it comes to proprietary vs. non proprietary advisors, I love to use two analogies to explain:

1. I'm Italian and I love to cook and eat great food. For all the grocery shoppers out there, this is probably my preferred analogy. As you walk into your favorite grocery store, you automatically glance down the twenty or so aisles. As you do, you realize that these aisles are almost empty. Walking down isle one, you see that there is a small portion of items on the far left bottom shelf. You gaze down and see that this is the store brand only section for ketchup and mustard products. Your favorite type of ketchup is a specialty brand for your favorite Italian meatloaf recipe; so, you move on. Walking down the second isle, there is a small selection of store brand spice and coffee choices. Again, you move on. Eventually, the realization comes to mind that the only choice you have in this

entire facility is **store brand proprietary products**…one choice. Why is that? Well it's simple, it's all about profit dollars and where this company make the largest percentage. It's not about offering you the *best* product…it's about company return on investment. **(ROI)** How can you benefit from the usage of a submarine type investment when it is not even offered?

2. Ladies, think about this one: You are invited to a ball at the White House. The dress you have is breathtaking; however, you require a new pair or snazzy shoes. So you go to a very substantial and reputable department store in town. You feel that they will supply you with the most options. As you walk in, you see a representative at the front door who walks you over to the lady's shoe section. You're dumbfounded because there are only two choices; one is a huge pair of shiny leather steel-toed army boots, and the other is a wild colored pair of women's snow boots. This representative informs you that these will come in your size and look fabulous! The salesman easily dismisses your questions and directs you, quite forcefully to buy the army boots. The ironic thing is that this boot is a size 15 … he says **"one size fits all ma'am."**

These analogies were exaggerations, but this is the same situation in the proprietary world of Investment and Retirement Planning. When you walk into a firm, you shouldn't be surprised that they would rather have you choose that one company product. The basis for their profit dollars is substantially built into their proprietary product line. You would not be pleased in a pair of black army boots with a spectacular red cocktail dress at a Presidential Gala: and you will not be satisfied settling for a generic-brand product that does not meet your needs—so why would anyone think you would be happy with just the small selection of products that a single firm offers. How can this company design one product to fit all? *They can't.*

I don't want to make this seem too humorous; however, for the serious retiree, **THIS IS A BIG DEAL!** Why wouldn't you want to look at one hundred ideas? Not just one or two. Why wouldn't you want to find out the full selection of investments so that your retirement is a success? Not just a few. Do you really want your financial future to be a struggle because you never got a chance to see all the available options? I hope not.

Putting the Client ~~First~~ Last

Here is the cold hard truth. In big proprietary firms, you don't come first. You can't. There is the representative, trying to get his commission—which is fine; but, then there is a Branch Manager, also trying to get his/her commission. Then there is the stock holder, you guessed it ... wanting their cut, and between them, there is likely a bunch of middle managers, and then the CEO. The CEO expects a BIG bonus. Then there is overhead, including the pricey rent or mortgage on the building, the utilities, the building maintenance fee, landscaping, and parking lot. Don't forget about the cost of hundreds of desks, computers, coffee makers, and copy machines. This is a BUSINESS in the true sense of the word; and your investments and you ... well, you are what make all that possible. Look below to see where you're positioned on this proprietary chart...not only on the bottom ... but the smallest and most insignificant portion.

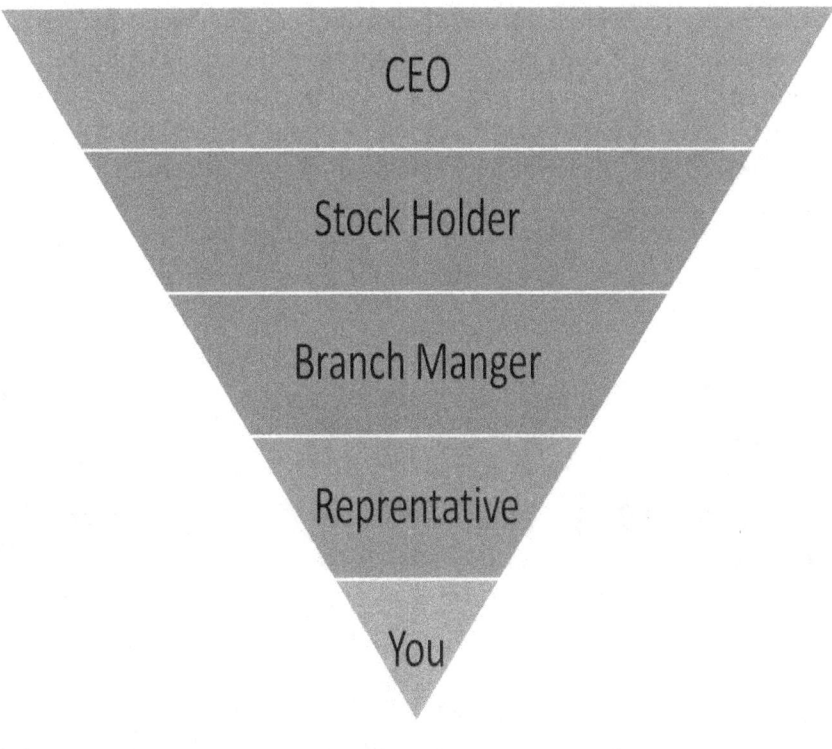

The Independent Advisor Associate is the Answer

Some representatives are just insurance agents selling products with little ability to offer advice as to all the options and usages. They hold limited licenses. They can be either proprietary or non-proprietary. These limits do not allow them to show or promote the many options that may help an investor get to the next level when it comes to the investment world. They have no ability to show a speedboat, submarine, or aircraft carrier. Their modern day sailboat can be also questionable because of the limited speed. It's very slow.

Today is a special time for most retirees and soon-to-be retirees because they can establish a relationship with an independent advisory associate. With limited dollars they can invest in a way; that just twenty years ago, would have taken millions of dollars to do. The programs of today contain a multitude of options to help investors stay ahead of the game. Go for 3 in 1: hire a CFP® professional, independent and non-proprietary, and an Advisory Associate. By doing this; the advisor may not only be qualified to show a multiple of boats, but also be better suited to show you the many opportunities in the investment world of today. They can become a true partner helping to guide you through your second half of life.

CHAPTER 9

All Bets are Off ... Bear Markets Will Destroy Your Retirement

The following chapter is very important because it shows the variables involved in retirement success and the importance of positive yearly investment returns. I will attempt to stress the fact that negative "Sequence of Returns" can destroy a great retirement plan. I want to give a special thanks to Jeff Manry, CFP* professional and his company, Betavest. His concepts helped me to see the truth; and hopefully, they'll help you.

This chapter will discuss the following areas:

- When it Comes to Retirement and Bear Markets...All Bets Are Off
- Certainty vs. Uncertainty
- Sequence of Returns and Uncertainty
- Your Outcome
- Level of Success
- Your Homework
- Needs vs. Wants Revisited

When it Comes to Retirement and Bear Markets... All Bets Are Off.

It can be devastating when the markets fall and this can have a profound negative impact on your retirement plan. Many Americans are very aware of this today—yet aren't sure what to do. Remember the famous movie *A Few Good Men*? Near the end, there is a moment when Jack

Nicholson dramatically utters the words: **"you can't handle the truth."** That is so exhaustive to me. My own research shows that looking at just the past seventy years on average, approximately every six years we average a dramatic 30% downturn. If the average American wishes to live 24 years (or more) in retirement (age 60-84), that means they, and their retirement savings, may experience **4** large possible downswings. Can you handle the truth? Bear markets happen –and they can be devastating.

P/E Ratios of the S&P 500 During Bear Markets

Start of Down Cycle	End of Down Cycle	Decline on P/E of S&P500	Fall in Price of S&P 500
05/29/1946	06/14/1949	-73%	-29%
08/02/1956	10/23/1957	-19%	-21%
12/12/1961	06/27/1962	-35%	-28%
02/09/1966	10/10/1966	-27%	-22%
11/29/1968	05/27/1970	-34%	-36%
01/11/1973	10/04/1974	-64%	-48%
11/28/1980	08/13/1982	-25%	-27%
08/25/1987	12/07/1987	-40%	-34%
07/16/1990	10/12/1990	-22%	-20%
03/24/2000	10/10/2002	-18%	-49%
10/09/2007	3/09/2009	-22%	-57%

Source: Standard & Poor's. The S&P 500 is an unmanaged index of stocks considered to be representative of the large-capitalization U.S. stock market. For the period December 31, 1939 to December 31, 2009. Investors cannot invest directly in an index. Past performance does not guarantee future results.

In early 2004, I had been in countless meetings with many of the top advisors in the United States. As I sat in meeting after meeting listening to experts discuss the current market conditions, I couldn't help but shake my head. It seemed that no one wanted to find out how to help our clients avoid loss and stop the bleeding. I felt as if I was riding in a sinking row boat with a hole as big as a bowling ball in it. While the boat was going down, all that I had to bail the water out was a little tablespoon … it was a ridiculous impossibility.

I have to laugh at the investment world, they never want to risk getting in front of the problem (the snowball)—opting to try to fix the mess after it is over.

At that same time, I had the pleasure of meeting Jeff Manry, CFP˚ professional at a Prudential seminar in Charlotte, N.C. Jeff started his company, BETAVEST in 2000 and had multiple years of experience. His ideas were new, innovative, and a breath of fresh air. As he was presenting his software, I sat back in my chair and knew exactly where he was going. To my dismay, many advisors in the room seemed untouched and undaunted by the information. I blame this on what I call **"big business brain washing."** A type of follow our rule mentality that expresses an "our way is the only way" thought from top management. The Advisor Associates were being brainwashed—believing just what they were told, and never being held accountable for finding out the truth. I think that this chapter may surprise many readers because of the big business ideology of today and how the proprietary world really works.

That day, Jeff asked us the following questions:

1) If a hypothetical diversified large company stock portfolio averaged 12% per year over the last 65 years, what would you expect it to average per year during the next 25 years?

2) Assuming you invested your retirement funds in the above stock portfolio at the beginning of a 25 year retirement period during which you anticipate your income need to increase by 3.5% annually, how much would you consider a reasonable first year withdrawal percentage from your portfolio?

3) As you near retirement and during retirement, it is important to reduce your stock market exposure and increase your bond and CD exposure. True or False?

4) If three people invest the same amount of money at the same time each using one of three different investments that all averaged 10% for 10 years, and they deposit and withdraw the same amount at the same time, do they end up with the same value at the end of the period?

Go through these slowly and think about the first answer that comes to mind. I'll give you the answers later. The next few pages should be enlightening.

Certainty vs. Uncertainty

The following compares certainty, no risk, to uncertainty, high risk. Certainty is defined as a Certificate of Deposit and Uncertainty as Diversified Stocks.

The certainty of CDs on cash vs. the uncertainty of the stock market.

In order to understand Certainty vs. Uncertainty, the readers should look at a main mathematical approach: This is just one example of possibilities with returns.

Certainty: Certificates of Deposit	Uncertainty: Diversified Stocks
More Predictable End Values & End Date	Unpredictable End Values & End Date
No Negative Returns or Investment Losses	May Incur Negative Returns or Investment Losses
Historically Poor Inflation Protection	Historically Better Inflation Protection
Simple Management	Advancement Management
FDIC* Principle Protection	No Principal Guarantee
May Increase Probability of Capital Depletion**	May Reduce Probability of Capital Depletion**
Average Return of 3%	Average Return of 10%
Inflation -4%	Inflation -4%
-1% Net Growth Yearly	6% Net Growth Yearly

*FDIC: An Independent agency created by congress in 1933, the FDIC supervises banks, insures deposits up to $100,000 and helps maintain a stable and sound banking system.
** Probability of capital depletion is dependent upon amount of withdrawal and length of withdrawal period.

Overall, Government Bonds, T Bills, and Certificates of Deposit (CD) represent a legal obligation of the government, meaning the interest and principal is generally paid even in a weak economy. For the holder of Government bonds, CDs or T-bills, the loss of principal could occur, in the extremely rare situation, the issuing government failed to recognize its debt obligations. This means that bonds, CD's, and T-bills are generally less risky investments than stocks. As a result, due to the lower risk involved, bond returns are usually lower than stock returns. Note that bonds also face market risk. A recession or inflation affects the bond markets. Sometimes market forces will cause interest rates to rise, leaving the investor holding a bond with a value much lower than the face value. Although stocks may produce returns that may be higher than bonds, T-bills, or CD's, there is an inherit risk of investing in stocks which may result in a loss of value or principal.

Sequence of Return and Uncertainty

The sequence of returns and average return are two different things. An early bear market occurring during a person's retirement will kill the investment if it isn't properly allocated. Take the following example:

Example A: (Lump Sum) $100,000 Original Investment Buy & Hold for 10 years.
Example B: (The Saver) $10,000 deposit per year for 10 years.
Example C: (The Spender) $100,000 Original Investment with annual withdrawal of 6% at the end of the year, with 3.5% annual withdrawal increase for 10 years.

Annual Returns

Portfolio A	10	10	10	10	10	10	10	10	10	10	**10% Average**
Portfolio B	-20	-10	-5	30	25	20	30	10	-5	25	**10% Average**
Portfolio C	35	25	30	20	15	10	5	-8	-15	-17	**10% Average**
Portfolio D	12	18	17	14	-8	-18	30	15	25	-25	**8% Average**

As you can see – Portfolios A, B & C all have the same average, 10%. But the year to year differences in annual returns varies wildly.

Investment Results

	Portfolio A		Portfolio B		Portfolio C		Portfolio D	
	End Value	Return	End Value	Return	End Value	Return	End Value	Return
Example A	$259,370	10%	$226,496	8.52%	$226,951	8.54%	$186,382	6.5%
Example B	$175,312	10%	$215,801	13.6%	$108,097	1.41%	$125,174	4.1%
Example C	$150,161	10%	$88,862	6.1%	$161,203	10.58%	105,747	7.3%

Despite the fact that this is hypothetical and you should not draw any conclusions about particular investments from these illustrations, you <u>can</u> see how sequence and range of return, or how much and when you deposit or withdraw, can be more critical to your success than your "average rate of return." Example B and Portfolio B show a return of 13.6% vs. 10%. Example B and Portfolio C shows a return of 1.41% vs. 10%. Sequence of returns and average returns are like peanut butter and jelly; much different, but they can go together to make a sandwich. Sequence is the peanut butter, it's much more important when you retire and no one wants just a jelly sandwich.

A large sum put into the market can be more advantageous than little pieces going in systematically, that's obvious. Take an average client account that is over $500,000. Serious people that have already saved don't want to have a large market loss (not that anyone does). If you look at Example B and Portfolio B, a systematic saver actually did better because in the early years they only had a small amount in the market. I had many clients in early 2000 through 2002 that invested their entire retirement portfolios. The "submarine" I used at that time was a systematic movement into various stock exposures monthly. Some of these accounts returned a positive 15% on average as the market was down 50% total. This is a great way to take a conservative investor in a volatile market and help them invest slowly.

The down side is that if the market were to be in a great position ... a "speedboat" would have done well for Example A and Portfolio C. This would have had to be managed well and pulled out of the market before the losses of year 7-10. (This shows another reason to guarantee the boat.) I know it's impossible to time the markets and that's why a submarine may ride on top of the ocean some days and hide underwater others. There are truly times when investing 100% in the market is like riding in a boat in a storm ... why would one do that? I believe in most cases, a mixture of boats is required to handle the up and down years. How does your fleet look?

Let me mention again the guarantees along with the speedboat in Example A and Portfolio C. Talk to a CFP® professional about how these programs work. This account would have grown to $412,931 by year 11 by using a guarantee of yearly step up along with a 6% yearly growth ... $412,931 vs. $226,917 ... what a difference! For the CPAs in the world that only see the trees and not the forests; I believe the small fee to guarantee future income is a small price to pay. At age 50 and above...when retirement becomes an important issue... the monthly income check that a retiree counts on... each and every month for the rest of their life... is the most important thing in the world. "Peace of mind" and security of income helps retirees to live carefree and happy.

At the end of the day; the most important point of these last two pages is that after an individual turns age 50, a large negative return will be devastating to the portfolio. Negative returns just prior to retirement or in the initial years of retirement can be a game changer. (Note: this does not take into account any fees, or taxes, but does assume that withdrawals and deposits were made at the beginning of each year.) You need to work with your Financial Professional – whom you trust and who cares about your success to be able to choose the right course of action for you.

A quick story: I sat with three very successful businessmen in the late nineties. Totally, they had managed to save over $4,000,000 in their 401K accounts. I discussed my concepts at a lunch meeting about diversifying and owning different types of vehicles. To my dismay, they just laughed at me. They literally laughed at me. At that time, they had their entire portfolio mix into just **one** company stock. **WHAT A SHAME!** Ten years later, I ran into one of them near Southpark Mall in Charlotte, NC and he began to tell me that they were all currently looking for work. How sad is that? Their retirement accounts had been devastated; but, if they had taken that small piece of advice, the future lives of three families could have been changed forever.

		Paul			Meghan	
Age	Return Amt	Withdrawal at start of year	Account Value	Return Amount	Withdrawal at start of year	Account Value
65			$500,000			$500,000
66	-10.14%	$25,000	$500,000	3.81%	$25,000	$500,000
67	-13.04%	$25,750	$426,835	12.8%	$25,750	$493,098
68	-23.37%	$26,523	$348,784	3.01%	$26,523	$527,168
69	17.23%	$27,318	$236,949	9%	$27,318	$515,715
70	1.41%	$28,138	$257,473	26.39%	$28,138	$532,352
71	26.38%	$28,982	$232,569	19.51%	$28,982	$637,277
72	15.32%	$29,851	$257,293	26.67%	$29,851	$726,974
73	2.59%	$30,747	$262,286	31.02%	$30,747	$883,045
74	12.41%	$31,669	$237,536	20.27%	$31,669	$1,116,681
75	27.25%	$32,619	$231,415	34.11%	$32,619	$1,304,943
76	-6.58%	$33,598	$252,967	-1.47%	$33,598	$1,706,314

77	26.35%	$34,606	$204,935	7.03%	$34,606	$1,648,127
78	4.47%	$35,644	$215,210	4.47%	$35,644	$1,726,951
79	7.03%	$36,713	$187,593	26.35%	$36,713	$1,766,909
80	-1.47%	$37,815	$161,486	-6.58%	$37,815	$2,186,102
81	34.11%	$38,949	$121,854	27.25%	$38,949	$2,006,930
82	20.27%	$40,118	$111,183	12.41%	$40,118	$2,504,255
83	31.02%	$41,321	$85,471	2.59%	$41,321	$2,769,937
84	26.67%	$42,561	$57,845	15.32%	$42,561	$2,799,287
85	19.51%	$42,838	$19,360	26.38%	$43,838	$3,179,057
86	26.39%	-	-	1.41%	$45,153	$3,962,290
87	9%			-17.23%	$46,507	$3,972,369
88	3.01%			-23.37%	$47,903	$4,602,288
89	12.80%			-13.04%	$49,340	$3,490,025
90	3.81%			-10.14%	$50,820	$2,992,020

Compound Average Annual Return	Total Withdrawal
9.87%	$671,759

Compound Average Annual Return	Total Withdrawal
9.87%	$911,482

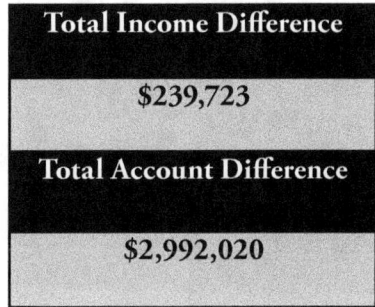

Total Income Difference

$239,723

Total Account Difference

$2,992,020

In this chart, you can see two investors that started with the same amount of money. Paul runs out at age 86 while Meghan keeps going! Both withdrew 5% each year and inflation stayed steady at 3%. Both averaged 9.87% annual return, but had much different results based on the "**sequence of returns**." The early negative years killed Paul's investments and retirement future.

The market returns, just prior to and in the initial years of retirement, can have a dramatic effect on your ability to support yourself throughout the last years of your life! The sequence of returns is so very important at this stage. The total account difference of $2,992,020 is dramatic and significant. For those of you that are taking this lightly … you better wake up. This is the most important variable in your life going forward that you can't control … position your boats correctly … **Good Luck!**

Your Outcome

Your outcome is a mixture of Asset Allocation which is accomplished by your Financial Professional, your deposits and withdrawals which is accomplished by you, and the "sequence of returns" which is accomplished by the markets.

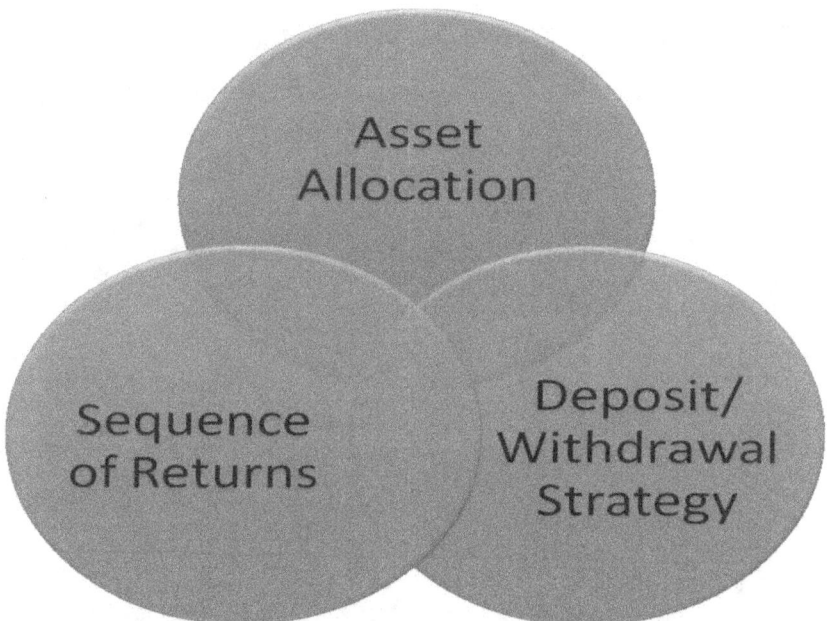

Level of Success

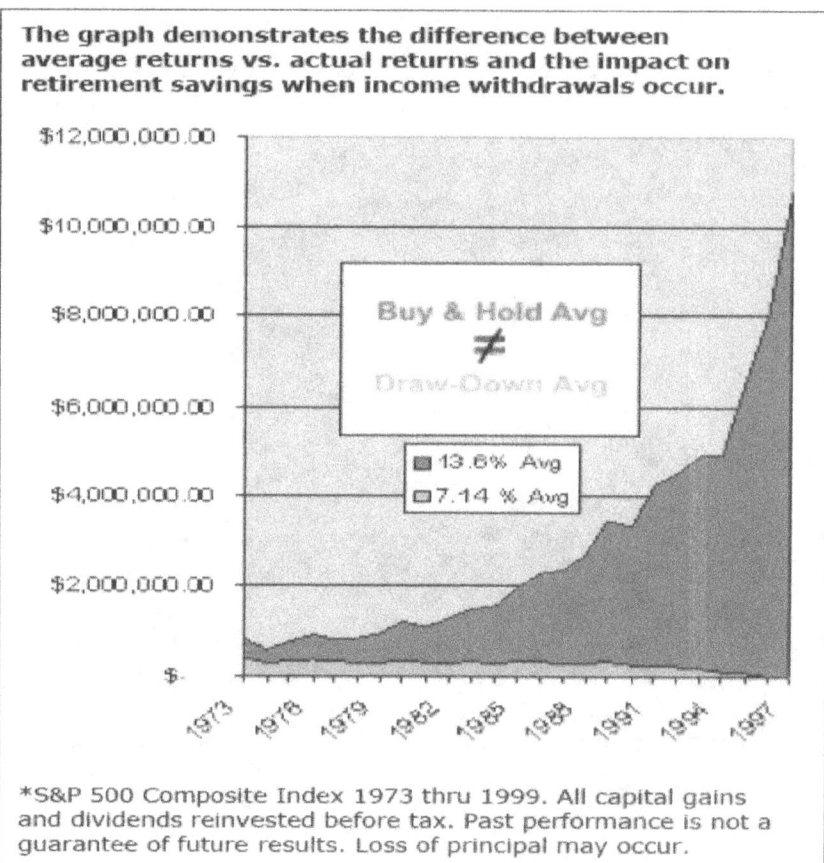

The graph demonstrates the difference between average returns vs. actual returns and the impact on retirement savings when income withdrawals occur.

Buy & Hold Avg ≠ Draw-Down Avg

■ 13.6% Avg
□ 7.14 % Avg

*S&P 500 Composite Index 1973 thru 1999. All capital gains and dividends reinvested before tax. Past performance is not a guarantee of future results. Loss of principal may occur.

Wow! Between the years 1973 thru 1999 the average annual rate of return for the S&P 500 equaled **13.6%.** It would appear as though an annual withdrawal of 6% increasing 3 ½ % annually would have been sustainable. However, because of the actual annual "sequence of returns," the original retirement savings would have depleted in 1997 and compounded at **7.14%.** Wow, $365,000 would have grown to over **$10,000,000 vs. zero** in retirement taking withdrawals ... Do you think finding a way to guarantee these accounts and income may be important? **I certainly hope that you've read this paragraph carefully ... Retirees that have started withdrawals or soon-to-be retirees that plan on taking withdrawals in the near future must have their "fleet established." Plan or parish!**

Your Homework

Congratulations, you're almost done. If you've learned anything at all; it's that planning ahead and choosing the correct boats is very important for your retirement future. You must have a game plan for surviving the ups and downs of the stock market.

So, what is the next step? Now it's time to go over your personal situation and give some ideas of how to plan for the "second half of your life." Keep in mind that life is a **journey** and not a **destination.** Retirement will be a moving target for most. In retirement, you will probably have to adjust your income needs based on the current market conditions. If the year that you wish to go to Hawaii is the year that the stock market falls 40% ... you may want to wait until the market performance is in the positive, and vice versa. In a good year ... go have a little fun!

Many American families are clueless when it comes to their retirement budget. (To be honest, many American families are clueless when it comes to budgeting at all!) I know that many books and planners have a percentage number that they wish to use; but let's first go about this the old fashion way and write the numbers down. This is why I have titled this section: **Your Homework.**

Having this information will be very advantageous when you hire a Financial Professional. You'll be ahead of the game by making some important considerations.

I want to stress that writing down your goals and budget will produce a basic variable of **NEEDS, WANTS, and WISHES.** Write them down accordingly because living and enjoying a normal lifestyle is more important than buying a new car or new home.

A risk analysis is very important when deciding your basic investment strategy. Think deep inside your heart and decide how you feel about the risk vs. reward scenario. If your needs, wants, and wishes are so great that you have to be more aggressive than you feel you should...you may want to readjust your goals. You're the one that has to sleep at night.

We know that **"time"** is what makes the markets work efficiently and unfortunately **"time"** is a commodity that retirees cannot have. "**Tomorrow is promised to no one**." We also know that by being too conservative, many will outlive their cash. Waking up at age 75 and looking at a zero balance in your investment account is a horrible fate that many may possibly see. The following points may help you form your budget.

BUDGET
**Fill in the blanks. What do you spend
monthly/yearly on the following?
Are they "Needs" or "Wants"?**

Mortgages:

Equity Line:

Special Purchases:

Real Estate Taxes:

Insurance: (Home, Auto, Life, Health)

Homeowners and/or Club or Association Fees:

Phone:

Water:

Electricity:

Sewer:

Gas:

Garbage:

Food: (groceries)

Dining Out:

Television:

Internet:

Lawn Care:

Household Misc.:

Pest Control:

Auto Loans:

General Household Maintenance:

Auto Maintenance:

Fuel:

Personal Property Tax:

Recreation:

Bank Fees:

Alimony:

Child Support:

Elder Care:

Charity/Donations:

Clothing:

Entertainment:

Pets: (grooming, vet, pet food, etc.)

Hobbies:

Child/Grandchild Education Accounts:

Travel:

Medical Expenses:

Long Term/ End of Life Expenses:

Life Insurance:

Debts:

Other: (List)

Add 10% for Unanticipated Expenses:

Do you have any additional expenses that are not accounted for above? Can you expand any of these categories such as travel, family, and vacation? Look at what you are spending now.

What percentage of your money is going to needs vs. wants?

NEST EGG
Fill in the blanks. List the following assets and income:

Social Security:

Home Equity:

Pension:

Total Monthly Income:

401K:

Cash Out Pension:

Company Stock:

Other Company Cash Benefit:

IRA Accounts:

Total Taxable Retirement Accounts:

Roth IRA Accounts:

Non Qualified Annuities:

Cash Life Insurance:

Mutual Funds:

Stocks:

Bonds:

Muni Bonds:

Cash:

Take these numbers to your CFP* professional along with your Needs and Wants Analysis. Now you will know the true picture of your retirement future (good or bad). This will help you to design a game plan to live a great second half of life.

Needs vs. Wants Revisited

Many "needs and wants" are easy to define. Put plainly we need toilet paper, but we want the double thick, extra soft rolls. However, when it comes to what we need and want in our retirement years, it can get a little more complicated.

I recommend that you look at your current household expenses including medical, groceries, utilities, mortgages, vehicles, clothing budget, prescriptions, insurance, etc., from this chapter. As much as we may want to simplify our lives in retirement, I have rarely seen anyone that wants to live on less income in retirement than they did in their working years. This is the essentials. These are your needs.

Let's take a quick look at your wants. Retirement is supposed to be a time of experiencing that which we couldn't during our working lives because of time and resources. None of this is important if we don't have the money to pay for the things we actually need, i.e. toilet paper!

It may also help to create 4 lists on a separate piece of paper with this information: needs, short-term wishes, long term wishes, and emergencies. What are the budget numbers? These long-term wishes can be your legacy, such as the money you leave in a trust for your children. The emergencies will be things that would be needed in a family crisis situation: the divorce of a child, the death of a spouse, or a natural disaster. These are things that we of course, do not want to think about - but it is better to be prepared than be surprised. Family crises happen. And having a contingency plan so that this does not affect your retirement will save you from having to give up on some of those wishes and wants … or worse, needs.

Also, you may want to plan trips and adventures in your early **"Go Go"** or **"Slow Go"** days. This may require using some of the vacation assets early while you can truly enjoy yourselves. Many individuals after reaching their late seventies become fearful of travel and don't seem to enjoy it as much as they once did.

CHAPTER 10

Planning for the Future

Now that you're about to finish this book, take all of this information that you have organized to your independent CFP® professional, whom you trust and believe will be a great partner going forward. He can then look at your entire array of needs and wants to give you a full picture of your future. You may need to sacrifice some wants now; so that you can have all of your wishes, later. In the end, this will be worth it. The more time you can spend in the preparation process; the longer you can have the kind of retirement, and hopefully legacy, that you have always dreamed and hoped for..

This chapter will discuss the following areas:

- The Markets Today
- Frugality
- Now What?
- The Post-Retirement Blues
- The Magic Moment
- I'll Take Five Pieces of Pie
- What is Your Value
- Preparing for the Transition

The Markets Today

Let's discuss some ideas about the psychology of the markets today. A great question to ask yourself involving the stock market today: **"will I survive the next stock market crash?"** It makes you think, doesn't it? Currently, we are on a six year run; but you'll hopefully see a multiple of BULL and BEAR markets in your lifetime. This is the way it works: and don't kid yourself…….. it always will.

How many of my readers believe we're due for some kind of correction at this time? I think most of you do. But, for the readers that have almost finished this book…you already know. You're prepared and mentally planning on how to control your retirement future going forward, thinking about what types of boats you should own, and strategizing for "that day." After all, *"What if You Live?"*

If you're age twenty, you can ride this roller coaster of a stock market for a while and just hold on. You have a forty year time span before retirement. **(Yes, you have TIME.)** If you're age fifty five and want to retire at sixty and … I mean … **retire at sixty** … watch out. I don't know the specifics or your personal life; but for many, maintaining a lifestyle and comfort level through retirement is very important.

I want to discuss the term "selective hearing" compared to "selective memory." I think all of us understand the term "selective hearing" (especially when it comes to a discussion with our spouses) – yes … I am trying to be funny. Now, "selective memory" is also very important. Can any of the readers remember the low of the Dow Jones in 2009? Think about it … think about it … **6547.05** … and look where the number is today.

The emotion of the stock market from 2007 until 2009 was exhausting and so very real. The gut wrenching pain, which emotionally you could have "cut with a knife," truly hurt. The future of many families was on the line and for some … they retreated out of the stock market never to re-enter, thus missing the trend upward. These are the kind of individuals that tend to "buy high" and "sell low." Wow, what a mistake.

It is truly a double edge sword. A CFP® professional may help a client with their "modern day sailboat" and show them how to move back into the market at its low point when emotions are high (this may be difficult). And, on the other hand, try to explain to a client the possibility of investing more conservatively when the markets are at their highest risk. As you can visualize, our brains tend to help hide the pain, thus give us "selective memory." **Just one man's opinion.**

By reading this book, you now understand major market volatility and how much a market crash can change your world. Find a CFP® professional you trust, and plan your life going forward.

Frugality

This is a topic that is a must for retirees. I have seen it too many times. Please be careful when you retire....money can go quickly. We all understand that if the markets are doing well and your account is flying, you can spend a little extra. But, if the market is constant or down and your account is decreasing due to spending ... stop ... think first ... budget.

My clients that lived through "The Great Depression" are frugal **100 percent** of the time. They lived it (hungry, searching for food, seeing others struggle). Observing the pain that this era brought all of America, changed them forever. And it put a lasting impression on their soul. Sometimes I have to laugh when I have lunch or dinner with someone from that era in history. They totally finish their plate of food.......I mean totally clean their plate.

The **"Baby Boomers"** haven't seen this type of struggle. Their mental setup is totally different. Until you've lived through something that horrific, you won't understand it. Boomers will spend and spend and spend ... until it's all gone. I mean this sincerely ... **be Frugal when you retire!**

Now What?

Many people spend their adult lives planning for their retirement in some way or another. If you are one of the smart ones, you have done it with good decisions, a relationship with a Financial Professional, and sound investing. However, all of this financial planning does not account for one of the universal truths of retirement: when we retire—truly retire; our job is no longer who we are. We are just ... **retired.**

It is not uncommon to define ourselves by what we do. We see ourselves daily as this person...a coworker or boss...a manager or owner. This tends to define us and how we imagine our value. Some recent and upcoming retirees will have spent thirty years or more at a single company, or in a single profession. If you were a teacher, if you were a computer programmer, if you were a doctor ... what "are you" when you retire?

Just as important as planning to be able to live comfortably to meet your needs and wants in retirement, is planning for a positive emotional state of mind at retirement. All the money in the world will not make you happy if you aren't prepared for how retirement will affect how you, and others, see you. On a scale from 1 to 10, you are always a 10 ... **you better believe it!**

The Post-Retirement Blues

Ah – retirement! How many of us have spent hours daydreaming of just reading in the hammock. We see ourselves spending weekends on the boat without the responsibilities of the day-to-day grind of work. It is a glorious thought, isn't it? That is what we work for after all - the ability **not to work**! As the time for our retirement approaches, we ache for these days of ease and happiness. We have every expectation that they will come. We look excitedly at that future, and we should!

Yet, no one ever thinks of the grey and rainy days of retirement. Few people ever consider boredom, loneliness, and depression as possibilities during their retirement—but they should. By its nature, retirement does not have the hustle and bustle of the busy 9-5 workday life; and many of us tie our self worth to our jobs.

I know of one lovely couple who recently retired. They had been planning their retirement correctly for years and took early retirement (ages 53 & 55). Despite the economy immediately taking a dip right as they moved into their dream retirement home, they could keep their income stable. This couple was frugal throughout their younger years and made great decisions. They jumped into their retirement with excitement and optimism, ready to **"finally relax"**.

Now this couple had dreamed of traveling the world together and took a fantastic several-week-long trip to Europe to celebrate the next phase of life. They visited museums, ate in great restaurants, and walked hand-in-hand along the Champs-Élysées at midnight. They had a marvelous vacation. Then they spent the entire next summer—two full glorious months, visiting friends and grandchildren across the country. Then they got home, exhausted from the whirlwind travel to "settle into retirement."

The reality of retirement and current life spans are that you could easily be retired for 30 years or more. That is a long time to sit reading in a hammock, or sitting silently across the table from a spouse you don't know anymore. This couple, married for 35+ years finally had time, for the first time, to be together every day with no other demands on their time. There was no job to go to and no children to take care of. Even harder, they were in a new town, separated from the people that had helped shape their lives, and separated from the jobs that had given their days purpose. They moved from their friends and support systems for this new **"perfect"** retirement life.

Truth be told, the couple of which I wrote, was unhappy and lost. They didn't feel that they offered value in their community, nor had value to each other. They had a monthly income to pay the bills and do something extravagant every couple of years—a trip or a major purchase. However, day-to-day they had nothing to talk about, nothing to share, and nothing to work towards together. It did not take long for them both to find new jobs—her as a full-time volunteer, he as a teacher for a community college. Money was not a motivating factor—self-worth and identity where.

I see this often, so I always counsel my clients when doing their retirement planning to plan for the "every day." When you consider what you "want" in your retirement, don't forget that there will be the time when the travel is over (or in between), when you are sitting in that lovely dream retirement home by the lake, trying to figure out who you are and what value you have. The couple of whom I spoke was lucky—they could move onto a new way of defining themselves, and do so quickly; but not all are. Divorce is not uncommon in this time of life; depression is not uncommon either. So remember, you need to plan the financial parts of retirement, but also the spiritual, health, spousal, and family aspects of retirement as well. Your spouse is the most important piece of your pie.

That Magic Moment

There is great significance in savoring those important moments in time as we see them slipping away. Some of you may think that I'm crazy; however, looking back over my life, I would grasp as hard as I could to hold on to those special times with all of my might. Today, it hurts just thinking about them; but the memories are so important to me.

As a young adult, leaving the farm in Michigan and moving to North Carolina was a **"magic moment."** I drove past my home, then my grandparent's home, and watched them wave goodbye. I realized at that millisecond, that the time before their deaths would be limited. This was very hard to do considering that we had lived side by side my entire life; and now, I was moving to a better place. I was leaving behind my **"foundation."** My grandparents were the most loving and special people that I will have ever known. This bond that we had is impossible to reproduce and the memories are immeasurable.

The first time I met my wife was a **"magic moment."** She entered through a garden at her sister's rehearsal dinner and walked towards me. The sun was setting behind her, and I can remember her silhouette of a long dress and bowed hair as if it was yesterday. She almost glowed as she walked towards me. Yes, there is "love at first sight."

Of course, the birth of our children was a **"magic moment."** I was scared to death. What a moment! For you soon to be Dads out there ... enjoy the time. Your children will grow up so fast that you will see many magic moments that must be grasped and held onto.

The last time I saw my father happy and laughing was a **"magic moment."** He had been diagnosed with lung cancer two years earlier and gone through surgery. We were on a golf course in Denver, N.C. He had asked me to stand in because one of his players could not make it. I drove up into the parking lot and looked for his golf cart. He was driving towards me and I could tell by "the look and the feel in the air" that I would never see him happy and joyful again. He died two months later.

The moral of these stories is this: the world is full of joy and pain. Embrace the joy and tell the pain to "jump in a lake." Every second you embrace a moment and love someone is a time you will never forget. Even in the later years of life, you cannot only find new magic moments, but you can also remember the old ones.

I'll Take Five Pieces of Pie!

"Balance" has been a popular topic for years among the weary workaholic set, and their stressed out and frazzled lives. This concept is very important and perhaps more applicable to the modern day retiree. Your overall well-being can be divided into five "pieces of pie:" Spouse, Family, Health, Spiritual, and Financial. Find the passion in all of your pieces of life.

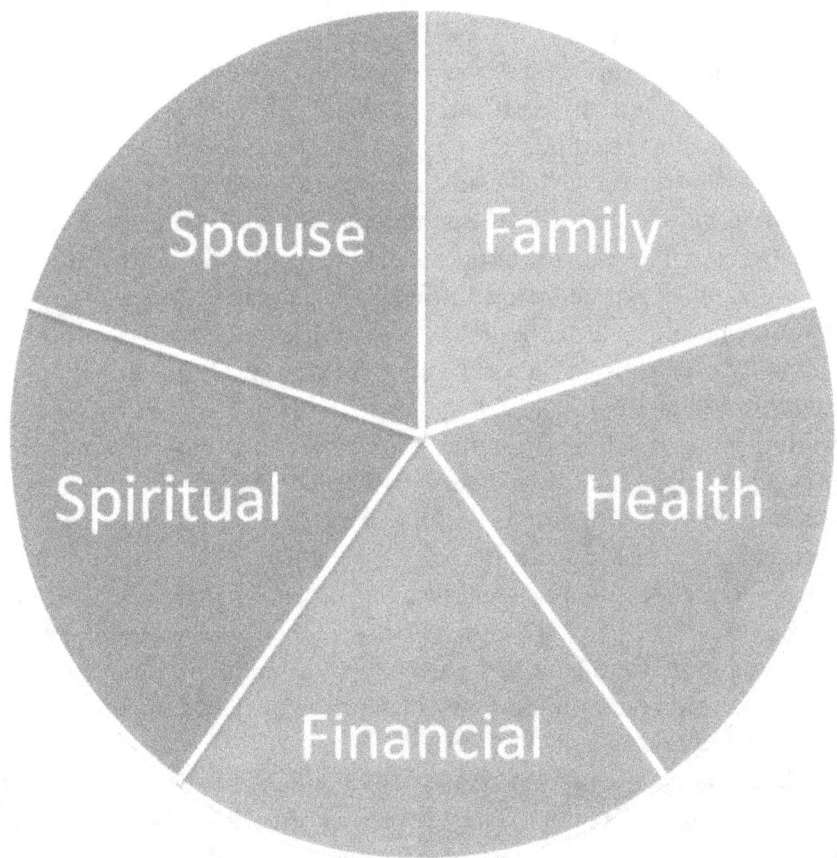

Spouse: If you are fortunate to go into retirement with a spouse, they should be a major, positive factor in your life. Devote time to your spouse in ways you may not have been able to do pre-retirement. Do the things that you have dreamed of doing together; and nurture your spouse's hobbies and interests, as if they were your own.

Family: There is no denying that your overall wellness can be affected dramatically by your relationships with family—and this includes your strong friendships as well. Remember, the people whom you "consider the family," can act as your support system, and you theirs. Many people dream of moving away to a tropical paradise when they retire; but then are miserable being so far away from family. What are you going to do to plan for a strong "friend and family" portion of your retirement? Now, this may mean finally moving close to the grand kids; or it may mean budgeting money for regular trips; but don't underestimate how this factor will make for a happy retirement.

Health: Dementia and Alzheimer's are major health issues that may turn your later years into a nightmare. We can anticipate some kind of difficulty in this world but it's tough to look into a mirror and imagine our last days as a total hell. I've seen many doctors discuss the fact that we now have the availability to check and find out if we are predestined to have either of these issues. The question: is it emotionally healthy to know these and other facts about our future? That's for you to decide!

Your health (and the health of your spouse!) needs to be a priority. If you have arthritis and a bad back then living in a climate that has 7 months of winter is a bad idea—you need to plan for a retirement in a warmer place! If you need routine medical care for a chronic condition, moving to the country, three hours away from a major medical center, is probably not in your best interest. One of my friends in Virginia just sold their home and moved to an area known for it's great hospitals because of his age. Regular exercise and healthy living become even more paramount in our retirement—so don't discount the value or budgeting for a gym membership, or fresh fruit and vegetables. Staying healthy will stave off depression and keep your physical self able to enjoy that financial nest-egg you have built up to … well … enjoy!

Spiritual: The emphasis on spiritual is different for everyone, and I very acutely recognize that. What are your spiritual goals? Well, it may be spending more time volunteering or it may mean leading a Bible Study. It may be attending seminary … or it may be something such as having a delivered home and life! It may be finding your purpose when it comes to helping children or building a church. We each define spirituality differently and that is a good thing. For the purposes of this process though, I just ask that you incorporate an aspect of communing with some kind of higher power in a way that gives you solace and peace—and that you make that an important part of your daily routine. Without this peace and fulfillment need met, happiness will elude you.

Financial: As you know by now, budgetary security can only help you in your goal of a happy retirement. Determining your needs and wants will help align your planning so that the other aspects of happiness: Spiritual, Health, Spouse and Family can be met. Find an independent Financial Professional that truly cares about your family and will help you succeed. Putting a plan in place so that you can maintain the lifestyle you expect will help you and your family reach their goals.

What is Your Value?

If you value yourself more for "what you do" rather than "who you are," you could end up with a zero balance in your emotional bank account when you choose to retire. The only way to guard against this is to spend the years leading up to your retirement recognizing how valuable you are as a person, not an employee. When I left my prior job years ago, I'll never forget the fact that no one bothered to call and wish me **"Good Luck."** I had spent fifty to sixty hours a week at that facility with a multiple of people that really didn't care about me. It was sad.

Think about this: who do you think has more self worth: a doctor who spent thirty years saving lives, or a waitress who went from job to job throughout her career? The answer is, as human beings, they have equal self worth. As they sit across the table from each other having a cup of coffee, they are equal in the **"eyes of God."** A doctor may retire with more net worth financially; but when he goes to retire, how will he define his value? Quite often, a person whose career profoundly shaped them will go from a perceived value of "very important" to a perceived value of "not important at all." This can have a devastating effect on our health, wellness, and relationship with others.

A paradigm shift in thinking must be done in the years leading up to retirement if you find that you value your self-worth in "what you are" instead of "who you are." The doctor may want to look at the other things he likes to do, is good at, or has in his life. He may wish to explore hobbies in his spare time, re-establish relationships with family and friends, or take classes at the community college.

As much as retirement is a time to do all those things you wish you had done; the time before retirement is when you need to think about what those things are, and start building towards the transition. You need to think of yourself as valuable regardless of what job you hold, or the people you have been working with. "What you did" goes away with retirement; but, your intrinsic value and importance do not.

Either way, find your passion in everything you do. This will help you find the true value of yourself and your future endeavors. Fill your pie with passion.

Preparing for the Transition

Planning is always a good idea—and the earlier the better. Take at least five years before your retirement start date to get your ducks in a row by sitting down with a CFP˚ professional. Hopefully these lists will help you prepare for your future. This is a quick list to keep for immediate usage in an envelope in a small fireproof safe close to your bed.

An Emergency List:

- **Medical Doctors List**
- **Pharmacist List**
- **Health Insurance Information**
- **Will**
- **Durable Healthcare Power of Attorney, Living Will**
- **CFP® professional and phone number**
- **Attorney and phone number**
- **Banker and phone number**
- **CPA and phone number**
- **Prescription Drugs**
- **Username and Passwords**
- **Bank Accounts and Safe Deposit Box, Register someone else to sign**

An Estate Planning List:

- **Three years Tax Returns**
- **Life Insurance and check Beneficiaries**
- **Retirement Accounts and check Beneficiaries**
- **Annuities and check Beneficiaries**
- **Will, Revocable Trusts, Financial Power of Attorney**
- **Ownership Documentation, Home, Land, Vehicle, Stocks, Bonds, Partnership, Corporate Agreements**
- **Escrow Mortgage Accounts, Loans to others**
- **List of Debts**
- **Marriage License**

- **Divorce Judgments and Decree, Distribution Sheet listing Bank Account Numbers that accompanied the Settlement to avoid disputes about ownership and payments due**
- **A Special Note to a Loved One**

Social Security: This is a big one. It is of utmost importance that you sit down with your CFP® professional and go over the many options of withdrawing Social Security. Not only is early withdrawals detrimental, but this will adversely effect your spouse in later years. If the male in the family plans on working through his late sixties and he can hold off on the benefit, his wife will usually receive a larger monthly check when he passes. The catch to this is that the family will still receive an income adjustment that will be lower than when both spouses were alive. **Wouldn't you know it?**

Clean-Up: Try to pay off any outstanding debts before you retire—especially any loans you took out against your retirement plans. If you don't, you will be paying them out of your savings or pension later. If you have credit card debt, home improvement loans, car loans, these should all either be paid off, or monitored carefully with your Financial Professional. These will be harder to take care of when you are on a "fixed income." It is most often best just to eliminate these expenses from your monthly budget by paying them down if you can.

Get Your Paperwork Done: Over the course of a lifetime, we can accumulate a lot of documents! Now is the time to organize and purge. Twelve months before you retire is a great time to start getting that paperwork in order. Don't be shy about throwing out the things that you don't need any more (that home depot receipt for the sprayer nozzle you bought in 1988 is not something you need to keep!). Organize old taxes, any important paperwork such as bank statements, mortgage and retirement fund information and any other records. Get your birth certificates, will, passports, and other identity paperwork all together, filed, and organized. This will help keep you on track, and in case of an emergency, will make it easier for family members to take care of whatever arises. Furthermore, if you are planning to move, this process will seriously cut down on what you need to take with you, and will allow you to easily put your hands on anything you need when you get to the new home.

Health Care: About six months to a year before your last day at work, check with your employer's benefits or HR department and ask them about how your health insurance will change upon your retirement. Some companies will extend full health coverage, but many will not. You may have to budget for new or supplementary insurance to meet your growing health needs as you age. By planning ahead, there will be no surprises, and you will be able to meet these additional expenses without taking them out of your retirement nest-egg. Obamacare has actually helped the individuals that wish to retire between the ages of 55 and 64. I think that the vote is still out when it comes to the healthcare benefits Medicare will provide going forward.

Create a Budget: Be sure to consider what your income sources will be after retirement. This can be a pension, Social Security, and personal savings and investments. Then create your budget well in advance so that you will be able to change it and adjust, in case you need to add additional expenses. If you do this a year beforehand, you should have enough of a margin to be able to prepare and adjust.

Make a New Tax Payment Plan: There are tax implications when you start drawing income from your investments. Work with your Financial Professional and your tax accountant on what forms you will have to submit and how to set up a payment plan so that you will be able to minimize taxes and maximize payments.

A Special Note for Women: Women should pay more attention to preparing for retirement than men in the years leading up to it. Death and divorce are common, and time off after having children actually cuts down the amount you earn so you may have to provide for yourself. Adequate preparation for any eventuality is a must. As a man, I can say that most males do go first when it comes to leaving this world; our spouses must be prepared.

CHAPTER 11

What if You Live?

How are Your Boats Positioned?

There is no way to be **"too"** prepared for retirement. If you carefully plan and take stock of your "needs and wants," go ahead and find the perfect partnership in a Financial Professional, then you will be on your way to a happy retirement.

This I know to be true: the average investor hasn't kept up with the average stock market returns by either chasing returns or making poor judgments as to where they invest. They took the advice of the **"talking heads"** and they underestimated bear markets and inflation. The average investor was optimistic about their money and pessimistic about their life expectancy! They also tend to buy high and sell low. This is not a good combination.

Many Americans don't know the difference between the fund choices in their investment accounts; let alone, the many vehicle options of today, and even more important, the WHY and the WHEN pertaining to their investment choices. They do not take the time to list their expenses or assets. They live their lives disorganized and lost, and then they retire—often unsuccessfully. You can't let this happen to you.

Ultimately, your retirement success will depend on your Financial Professional's chosen fleet along with the deposits and withdrawals that you make. Choosing this strategy and making appropriate adjustments is the reason that you work with an independent CFP® professional. The unpredictable future **"sequence of returns,"** will produce your uncertain future; yet with proper planning, your end value may give your family the resources necessary to comfortably live the retirement that you have always dreamed and hoped for.

Here is a chart demonstrating what could happen over your lifetime:

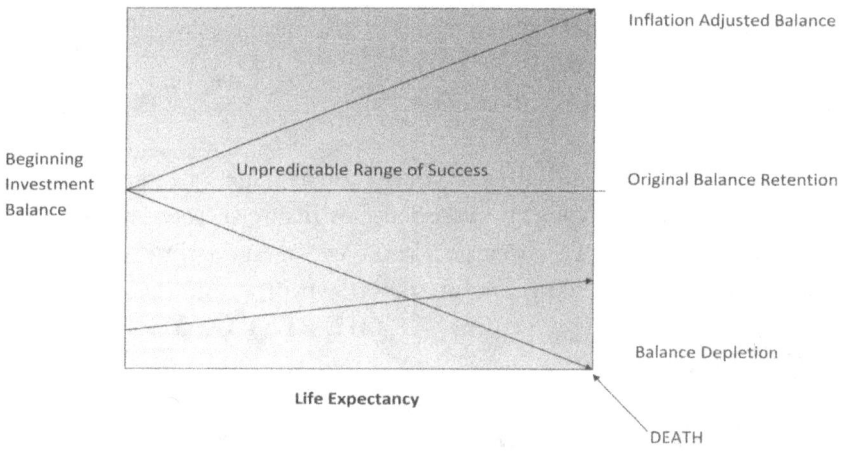

As you can see by looking at the chart, your worst case scenario should be to maintain income until death. If possible, it's very important to make sure your income level rises with inflation. But it's mandatory that you don't outlive your income. I know that it would be nice to leave the kids a nice chunk of change; but in today's world, it may not happen.

The primary goal is to generate an inflation adjusted income flow over your life expectancy with your final end value falling within the above range of success. If it were me, I would find a Financial Professional that believes in the new world concepts of a "Multiple Boat Theory" and guarantees the hell out of them. Why not invest in gold, China, or small company stocks and put risk reward into your future where the reward may be all that you see? Let the insurance company take the risk. Live your life without worry and have fun!

Bottom line: Guarantee your financial future and find someone you like and trust to work with. A successful retirement does not include running out of income. A happy retirement is one well planned and well timed! Check the boats you're in now and find out if a submarine or speedboat may help. Do you currently have a submarine, speedboat, aircraft carrier, or modern day sailboat in your fleet? I hope you're not in one of those sailboats from the 1400's—if so, watch out for the storms on the horizon!

I have two final questions for you:

If your home was paid for and there wasn't a mortgage, would you ever cancel your homeowner insurance? I will assume the answer is.....**NO!**

Then let me ask you the second question:

Assuming your IRA and 401K accounts are as large, or larger, than the value of your home, would it make sense to insure these assets as well? I hope you answered, **YES.** Because if you have taken the time to truly read this book and see the dangers of market downturns, and the importance of a positive "sequence of returns" ... **THE REST OF YOUR LIFE IS UP TO YOU!**

Because, after all ... *What if you live?*

The "What if you Life?" Quiz

Have you been reading carefully? Here are a few questions to ponder. Hint: If you are having trouble with any of them, hopefully your advisor can assist you!

1. If a hypothetical diversified large company stock portfolio averaged 12% per year over the past 65 years, what would you expect it to average per year during the next 25 years? **Unknown, can only estimate.**
2. Assuming you invested your retirement funds in the above stock portfolio at the beginning of a 25 year retirement period, during which you anticipate your income need to increase by 3.5% annually, how much would you consider as a reasonable first year withdrawal percentage from your portfolio? **Five percent or less.**
3. As you near retirement (and during retirement), it is important to reduce your stock market exposure and increase your bond and CD exposure. True or False? **It depends on your income need and for how long.**
4. If three people invest the same amount of money at the same time, each using one of three different investments that all averaged 10% for 10 years, and they deposit and withdraw the same amount at the same time, do they end up with the same value at the end of the period? **It depends on the sequence of returns.**

A Final Quote

A lovely quote about the finality of life

"There is a universal truth we all have to face, whether we want to or not, everything eventually ends. As much as I've looked forward to this day, I've always disliked endings. Last day of summer, the final chapter of a great book, parting ways with a close friend. But, endings are inevitable, Leaves fall, you close the book. You say goodbye. Today is one of those days for us. Today we say goodbye to everything that was familiar, everything that was comfortable. We're moving on. But just because we're leaving, and that hurts, there's some people who are so much a part of us, they'll be with us no matter what. They are our solid ground. Our North Star. And the small clear voice in our hearts that will be with us…always."

From the television series "Castle" performed by his daughter Alexis at her graduation

Resources & Suggested Reading:

- Society of Certified Senior Advisors. *Working With Seniors Health, Financial, and Social Issues: CSA, 2005.*
- Betavest Technologies, Inc. www.betavest.com
- Merriam-Webster. *The Merriam Webster Dictionary.* Merriam-Webster, 1997
- Sandler Sales Institute®
- Mark Zinder

CFP™, CERTIFIED FINANCIAL PLANNER™, and CFP (with flame logo)® are certification marks owned by the Certified Financial Planner Board of Standards, Inc. These marks are awarded to individuals who successfully complete the CFP Board's initial and ongoing certification requirements.